ELSEWHERE TEXTS

EDITED BY

GAYATRI CHAKRAVORTY SPIVAK AND HOSAM ABOUL-ELA

The series takes as its charge radical new directions in the engagement with the literary culture of the non-European. The point of departure here is the scandalous notion that the literary figure of the Global South is as human as the European, complex, subject to the dynamism of history, fluid, unrepresentable, and impossible either to essentialize or reduce to any glib counter essentialism.

As such, ELSEWHERE TEXTS emphasizes those aspects of this subject's dynamism that have been radically de-emphasized in the stock metropolitan representations. So, the series centers the intellectual dimension of literary culture elsewhere. The regions that Orientalists represented as non idea producing areas are revealed to be the opposite. Furthermore, modernity of ideas is engaged by the series' metatheoretical understanding of the process of translation, the mechanism through which the unfixed nature of intellectual work may be most fully acknowledged. Finally, ELSEWHERE TEXTS understands theory as commitment, emphasizing that genre of theoretical discourse which through its engagement—its heightened sense of the social power of ideas and rhetorics—calls into question the supposed abstract transcendence of the god terms 'theory', 'text', 'idea'. This engaged dimension of the elsewhere text insists on the historicism of theory, but at the same time forges a new intellectual globality embodied here in intellectual work translated for the critical traditions of Asia, Africa, the Caribbean and Latin America in all their diversity.

In My Heart

SOPHONIA MACHABE
MOFOKENG

TRANSLATED FROM THE SESOTHO BY **NHLANHLA MAAKE**

INTRODUCED BY **SIMON GIKANDI**

LONDON NEW YORK CALCUTTA

Seagull Books, 2021

Originally published as *Pelong ya Ka*
© Witwatersrand University Press, Johannesburg, 1962.

First published in English translation
by Seagull Books, 2021

'Elsewhere Texts: A General Introduction'
© Gayatri Chakravorty Spivak, 2021

'Introducing *Pelong ya ka*' © Simon Gikandi, 2021

Translator's Note and English translation
© Nhlanhla Maake, 2021

ISBN 978 0 8574 2 892 9

British Library Cataloguing-in-Publication Data
A catalogue record for this book is available from the British Library

Typeset by Seagull Books, Calcutta, India
Printed and bound by Versa Press, East Peoria, IL, USA

CONTENTS

ELSEWHERE TEXTS

A GENERAL INTRODUCTION

Gayatri Chakravorty Spivak

'Theory' is an English transcription of the Greek theorein. Corresponding words exist in the major European languages. Our series, 'Elsewhere Texts', works within these limits. 'Theory' has been creolized into innumerable languages. Yet the phenomenon of 'seeing or making visible correctly'—the meaning in Greek that will still suffice—does not necessarily relate to that word— 'theory'—in those languages. That describes the task of the editors of a translated series on theory in the world. How does 'theory' look elsewhere from the Euro-US? Since our texts are modern, there is often an at-least-implicit awareness that 'proper' theory looks different as the 'same' theory elsewhere.

Heidegger thinks that truth is destined to be thought by the man of 'Western Europe'.[1] Our series does not offer a legitimizing counter-essentialism. Take a look at the map and see how tiny Europe is, not even really a continent, but, as Derrida would say, a cap, a headland.[2] Such a tiny place, yet who can deny Derrida's

---

1 Martin Heidegger, *What is Called Thinking?* (Fred D. Wieck and J. Glenn Gray trans) (New York: Harper and Row, 1968).

description, which is an historical and empirical observation? Look at the tables of contents of the most popular critical anthologies, and you will see corroboration of the essentialist conviction that goes with the historical claim. The counter-essentialism is reflected in the choice of critics from 'the rest of the world,' and today's espousal of 'the global South'. Just being non-white is the counter-essence. An axiomatics for the other side, as Black Lives Matter points out.

The influential *Norton Anthology of Theory and Criticism* for example, lets in only Maimonides before the modern university system kicks in.[3] But, even if they had let in Khaled Ziadeh, Marta Lamas and Marilena Chaui, the material would have been determined by the epistemological procedures of that system.[4] Norton lets in W. E. B Du Bois, the first African-American to get a doctorate from Harvard, the man who felt that 'of the greatest importance was the opportunity which my *Wanderjahre* [wandering years] in Europe gave of looking at the world as a man and not simply from a narrow racial and provincial outlook.'[5] Du Bois emphatically claimed that the African-American was the best example of the subject of the Declaration of Independence (the Founding Fathers were standing in). It is therefore significant that here he claims to inhabit the persona of Wilhelm Meister, Goethe's hero, with a trajectory not fully reversed. Meister came to the United States to act out the

---

2 Jacques Derrida, *The Other Heading* (Pascale-Anne Brault and Michael B. Naas trans) (Bloomington: Indiana University Press, 1992).
3 Vincent B. Leitch (ed.), *The Norton Anthology of Theory and Criticism* (New York: Norton, 2010).
4 These authors were published by Palgrave in a series similar to this one, under the same editorial collaboration.
5 Cited in Henry Louis Gates, Jr., 'The Black Letters on the Sign: W. E. B. Du Bois and the Canon' in *The Oxford W. E. B. Du Bois* (New York: Oxford University Press, 2007), VOL. 8, p. *xvi*.

European Enlightenment in this new land—a trip described in Goethe's *Wilhelm Meisters Wanderjahre* (Wilhelm Meister's Travels)— a hope which Du Bois nuanced, perhaps as soon as his scholarship to the Friedrich Wilhelm University from the Slater Fund for the Education of Freedmen was canceled, the year after President Hayes' death, by a Standing Committee on Education chaired by a former Lieutenant Colonel in the Confederate Army, the army that had fought to retain slavery and the slave trade in the US Civil War. (Hayes himself destroyed the possibility of Reconstruction by the 1877 Compromise with the Southern Democrats in order to retain the Presidency of the United States.) Du Bois as a young man was critical of his racism but probably not aware of political details, as he was later.

In the *Norton Anthology*, we get Zora Neale Hurston (Columbia), Langston Hughes (Harlem Renaissance via Columbia), Frantz Fanon (University of Lyon), Chinua Achebe (University College, Ibadan; professor in the US), Stuart Hall (Oxford), Ngugi wa Thiong'o (Leeds; professor in the US), Taban Lo Liyong (Iowa), Henry Owuwor Anyuumba (Iowa), Spivak (Cornell), Houston Baker (UCLA), Gloria Anzaldua (UCSC), Homi Bhabha (Oxford), Barbara Christian (Columbia), Barbara Smith (Mount Holyoke), Henry Louis Gates, Jr (Cambridge), bell hooks (UCSC). The point I am making is not that these writers have not challenged Euro-centrism—it is that they are sabotaging from within. And this is a historical fact that must be turned around, so that there is a chance for widening the circle. Fanon stands out because he is the only one who clearly operated outside the Euro-US, though he was what Du Bois would call a Black European, literally fighting Europe, also from within, located in a geographical exterior. Yet one cannot help suspecting that the certificate of violence granted him by the French philosopher Jean-Paul Sartre had a hand in this.

(In the next most influential anthology, the rest-of-the world entries are almost identical, but for Audre Lorde [Columbia], Geraldine Heng [Cornell], Ania Loomba [Sussex], Chidi Okonkwo [University of Auckland], Jamaica Kincaid [Franconia and New School].[6] Again, Fanon is the only working 'outsider'. I am sure the general pattern is repeated everywhere. I have myself been so tokenized through my long work-life as representing 'Third World criticism' that I am particularly alive to the problem.[7])

Our position is against a rest-of-the-world counter-essentialism, which honours the history versus tradition opposition. We recognize that a hegemonic Euro–US series can only access work abroad that is continuous with Euro–US radicalism.[8] To open ourselves to what lies beyond is another kind of effort. Within the limits of our chosen task we focus, then, on another phenomenon.

The history of the last few centuries has produced patterns of bi-lateral resistance. The formation is typically my nation-state, my region, my cultural formation against 'the West'. These days there are global efforts at conferences, events, organizations, that typically take the form of the Euro–US at the centre, surrounded by a collection of 'other cultures' connected through the imperial languages,

---

6 Michael Ryan and Julie Rivkin, *Literary Theory: An Anthology* (Malden: Wiley Blackwell, 2004).

7 An example that has stayed with me over the years remains Diane Bell's excellent *Daughters of the Dreaming* (Minneapolis: University of Minnesota Press, 1993), which, in response to requests for inclusion of third-world material, put in Trin-ti Min-Ha and me, long-time faculty persons in prestigious United States universities!

8 This continuity and the discontinuous are beautifully staged in *Bamako* (2006), by Abderrahmane Sissako. Jean François Lyotard gave a clear articulation of the problem of discontinuity in *The Differend: Phrases in Dispute* (Georges Van den Abbeele trans.) (Minneapolis: University of Minnesota Press, 1988).

protected by a combination of sanctioned ignorance and superficial solidarities and an ignorance of the internal problems even when they are at these global functions.[9] The model is the fact and discipline of preservation. By the Nara document of 1994, it was insisted that preservation should be not only of built space but also of intangible cultural heritage. What started was the model that I have described above. It is now a tremendous capital-intensive fact of our world.

In and through our series, we want to combat this tendency. We want not only to present texts from different national origins to the US readership, but we want also to point out how each is singular in the philosophical sense, namely, universalizable, though never universal. We are not working for area-studies niche marketing, though the work is always of specialist quality. In the interest of creating a diversified collectivity outside of the English readership, a long-term feature might be periodic conferences bringing the authors together.

The story begins for me in a conversation with the Subaltern Studies collective in 1986, asking them if I could arrange the publication of a selection from their work because they were not available in the United States. A long-term preoccupation, then. To this was added Hosam Aboul-Ela's 2007 consolidation of a thought that was growing inside me: from the rest of the world, literary editors wanted fiction, poetry, drama—raw material. Theory came generally from 'us'. Seagull Books, the only publishing house based in South Asia with direct world distribution, and, unlike most

---

9 My most memorable experience was to encounter a Maori activist bookseller and an Indian feminist at such a convention, who had never heard of Frederick Douglass, where only in response to my questions did the South African participant admit to political problems with translation between indigenous languages, and the mainland Chinese participant to the barrier between Mandarin and Cantonese. Examples can be multiplied.

western conglomerates, uninterested in translations of theory not recognizable by the Eurocentric 'cosmopolitan' model, seems now the appropriate publisher.

In the intervening three decades, a small difference has imposed itself, the one I have been emphasizing so far, the justification for 'elsewhere.' Earlier I had felt that my brief within the profession was to share and show that the work overseas was really 'theoretical' by Western sizing. (I use the word 'size' here in the sense of pointure in Derrida.)[10] Hence 'strategic use of essentialism.' Now I also feel the reader must learn that 'theory' need not look the same everywhere, that for the independent mind too much training in producing the European model in stylistic detail might be a hindrance. In my teacher-training work in rural India, it is the illiterate man who understands things best because his considerable intelligence has not been hobbled by bad education or gender oppression. The lesson here is not that everyone should be illiterate, but that strong minds should not be ruined by bad education or imperatives to imitate.

The caution would apply to *Neighborhood and Boulevard* by Khaled Ziadeh (belonging to our earlier series, see note 4)—not bad education, obviously, but the imperative to imitate 'French Theory'.[11] Ziadeh, in spite of his time at the Sorbonne, was not tempted. He theorizes by space and repetition; Hosam Aboul-Ela's Introduction to that book walks us through it. There are plenty of people writing in Arabic who produce work competitive with the

---

10 I have discussed this in 'Inscription: Of Truth to Size' in *Outside in the Teaching Machine* (New York: Routledge, 2009), pp. 201–16.

11 I use this phrase with the French nationalist irony reflected in François Cusset, *French Theory: Foucault, Derrida, Deleuze et Cie et les mutations de la vie intellectuelle aux États-Unis* (Paris: Découverte, 2003), translated by Jeff Fort as *French Theory: How Foucault, Derrida, Deleuze, & Co. Transformed the Intellectual Life of the United States* (Minneapolis: University of Minnesota Press, 2008).

best in European-style 'theory'. Reading Ziadeh, as Aboul-Ela points out, we have to learn to recognize 'theory' in another guise. My own work profits from his account of the de-Ottomanization of the city by the French into an 'Islamic' space; because I think de-Ottomanization, still active in our time, has a history as old as the Fall of Constantinople, and, re-territorialized, backward into Byzantium. Today's Khilafat movement can be read as an example of how imperial historical violence can produce a counter-violence of no return.

Our series is young. I have described our goal with appropriate modesty: to translate theoretical material operating outside the Euro-US, not readily available to metropolitan readership but continuous with the episteme, even as 'hybridity' keeps the local elsewhere. Yet there are also singular enclaves in many places where teaching and thinking apparently take place in less continuous epistemic formation. To acquire texts from these enclaves would require the kind of preparation, partly traditionalist, partly anthropologistic, that I do not possess. Perhaps, if our initial forays succeed, we will be able to fling our net wider: particularly important in the context of sub-Saharan Africa, where strong theoretical writing in the imperial languages (also languages of Africa, of course) flourishes and holds influence. For theoretical writing in the indigenous languages, not necessarily imitating the European model, contained within internal conflict, avoiding the anthropologist in the name of tradition will be on our agenda, I had written earlier.

Towards A History of the National-Popular in Bolivia, by René Zavaleta Mercado was our inaugural text. The next was a continuation of the work that Zavaleta could not complete because of an early death. Luis Tapia Mealla, a political philosopher at the Development Sciences institute (CIDES) of the Universidad Mayor de San Andrés in La Paz, in his book *The Production of Local Knowledge*, broadens Zavaleta's method into the global applicability that it contained. The importance of this for today's world, where every nation-state is hierarchically constituted, cannot be over-emphasized.

The book you hold in your hand, *Pelong ya ka* by Sophonia M. Mofokeng (1962), translated from the Sesotho as *In My Heart* by Nhlanhla Maake, is the kind of text of which I wrote in connection with Khaled Ziadeh, where a writer trained in Eurocentric institutions up to the doctoral level, attempts to access the theoretical through laying claim to a different 'normality' that always proceeds asymptotically with our European bi-culturalism. We must learn to recognize this as 'theory'. If we forget Charlemagne's injunction to 'Christianize Aristotle', we can re-think Aristotle's insistence in the *Nicomachean Ethics* that theory is not research, as this kind of wisdom rather than the origin of Eurocentric hierarchy that I invoked at the opening of this introduction.

The text was suggested to me by Njabulo Ndebele, the first Black vice-chancellor of the University of Cape Town, a co-worker with Steve Biko, a novelist and a critic in his own right. He told me that his father had suggested this book to him in the 60s. Simon Gikandi has written a brilliant Introduction for this volume. He shares a bit in the predicament faced by us as we try to negotiate globality, on islands of signs ('learn the system and you'll have meaning') in an ocean of traces ('here be language'), for Sesotho is not his language. And as he pointed out, Njabulo's own language is Zulu. Why did his father recommend a Sesotho text? Are these gestures of an urge to Pan-Africanism? The cliché is to impose upon Africa the thickest identitarianism, in admiration or derision.

Gikandi encourages us to learn to flex our imaginations sufficiently to grasp that the statements in the text are not necessarily culturally marked, although we are now programmed to assume so. It is that we cannot understand them—a point worth making. He cites Njabulo Ndebele's exhortation to restore the ordinary, a distant echo of Bessie Head: 'As an African, he wanted to be just anyone.' It is a question of language learning. Language learnt, we would be able to tell class and space difference and the historical difference between the two utterances. Not a question of highlighting the diasporic native speaker, which we in the United States often mistake for touching the continent of Africa. It is happening in India as the NRI (non-resident Indian, Indian officialese for Euro-US-Austro/Canadian expats) sets the intellectual, electoral and economic tone.

The experience of the production of this book was for me enhanced by the extraordinary exchange between the translator, Nhlanhla Maake, who left the University of Witwatersrand to become the managing director of of a merchandising company, and Sopelekae Maithufi, the first reader. I learnt a great deal about the nature of the Sesotho idiom as well as the nuances of gendering in the language.

At our provocation in the Modern Language Association conventions, Luis Tapia, the second author in this series, had provided a theory of how different 'local'-s might today connect through intermediary recognition of the globality nuanced differently in each case. I cling to that intuition as I go through each rich text in our series.

To begin with, my understanding of an activist 'Task of the Editor' was as I have outlined above: to combat the bi-lateralism—my place and your Euro-US—that legitimizes Eurocentrism by reversal. Today this is complicated by the confrontation between nationalism and globalism. Can an elsewhere text supplement both?

Down the line, a translation is well under way of the collected literary writings of Paik Nak-Chung, the brilliant Korean public intellectual. He is important for our world because he grasps the 'literary' in all its worldliness; and philosophizes the possibilities for a way out of gated nation-states. Translation has begun on *Mononer Modhu*, a philosophical text by Arindam Chakrabarti which, in the best comparativist tradition, deconstructs European philosophizing into ways of thinking that it otherwise ignores. Also underway is *Gender, Context and the Politics of Writing*, by Dong Limin from China, a powerful critic of many accepted social gender paradigms

Our translators share with us the problems of translation for each unique text, at least hinting to the reader that, although the activity of translating is altogether pleasurable, to accept translations passively as a substitute for the 'original' closes doors. We will not give up the foolish hope that a careful translation, sharing problems, will lead to language-learning.

Read our series as a first step, then. Come to the projected conferences if they happen, where all of the authors and translators will gather, to ask: What is it to theorize elsewhere, in our world?

INTRODUCING *Pelong ya Ka*
Simon Gikandi

One of the great ironies surrounding the production of African
knowledge in the first half of the twentieth century was that,
even as colonial institutions sought to extend their hold over the
continent through a regime of documentation, a new generation of
Africans had embarked on a silent textual revolution whose goal
was nothing less than the rethinking of their identities and modes
of being in the age of empire. While they are barely acknowledged
in Euro/American accounts on the production of African knowledge, writers working in African languages are legendary among
their own communities of readers. In fact, writers such as Daniel
Fagunwa (Yoruba), Magema Fuze (Zulu), Gaakara Wanjau (Gikuyu),
Ham Mukasa (Buganda), Sol Plaatje (Tswana) and Thomas Mofolo
(Sesotho) were at the forefront of producing narratives in African
languages in the grey zone between the colonizer and the colonized.
Often confined to the role of native informants, or expelled from
the mission schools and churches that had created them in the first
place, these writers laid the foundation for the politics and poetics
of decolonization. Elsewhere, I have called these writers 'untutored'
intellectuals, not because they were uneducated but because they
operated outside the rules and practices that governed the production
of African knowledge within the authorized institution of the colonial

university.[1] They effectively created an African reading public on the margins of the colonial system. And if these writers have proven difficult to read or analyse within the colonial or postcolonial episteme, it is because their aspiration—the need to produce African knowledge, not in opposition to the colonial episteme but outside it—does not fit well with the binary discourse (the West and the Rest) that was cultivated by the nationalist elites produced by the colonial university.[2]

The 'untutored' intellectuals were, of course, privileged within the new colonial order: they were often the first in their communities to acquire literacy; they grew up in Christian households; they were educated at mostly mainstream Protestant missions; and they were surrounded by the aura that came with Westernization. But with few exceptions, these writers were also considered renegades from the institutions that had produced them as new, colonial subjects. They were often sent away from the mission because their works seemed too sympathetic to cultural practices—mostly witchcraft and magic—that were at odds with the civilizational mission of late colonialism; their evangelizing projects were praised by the missions, but their fictional or imaginative work was feared and often repressed.[3]

---

1 I discuss the cultural politics of early African writers in *Imagining Decolonization: African Literature and its Public 1890–1980* (forthcoming). For colonialism and the regime of documentation, see Sean Hawkins' *Writing and Colonialism in Northern Ghana: The Encounter Between the LoDagaa and 'the World on Paper'* (Toronto: University of Toronto Press, 2002), pp. 11–23.

2 This binary, common with postcolonial elites in the first decades of independence in Africa, was popularized by Chinweizu in *The West and the Rest of Us: White Predators, Black Slavers and the African Elite* (New York: Vintage, 1975).

3 At the Paris Evangelical Mission in Morija in Lesotho, to cite one prominent case, Thomas Mofolo was celebrated by missionaries for *Moeti oa*

S. Machabe Mofokeng's *Pelong ya Ka* belongs to this tradition of colonial renegades, but is marked by a crucial difference—it is a work produced by a member of the elite but in conversation with non-elite readers. Like the 'untutored' intellectuals mentioned above, Mofokeng assumed, often against colonial logic, that African languages could function as the basis of a systematic thinking of African Being amidst the chaos unleashed by colonization. But unlike these intellectuals, Mofokeng was tutored. Indeed, he was a product of several colonial institutions of higher education committed to chaperoning the New African into both the cultures and morals of Europe and the mastery of the disciplinary protocols that would domesticate European knowledge in an African context.[4] Given these credentials, it is strange that Mofokeng, one of the few blacks to have a PhD from a premier South African university in the Apartheid period, has not been admitted into the postcolonial institutions of interpretation. It is, in fact, peculiar that unlike E'skia Mphahlele, whose education and career was similar, Mofokeng was not—and has not yet—been recognized as a central figure in the shaping of African literature and its criticism.

Here, contrasts are informative: in 1957, Mphahlele submitted a thesis on 'The Non-European Character in South African English Fiction' for his MA to the University of South Africa. For most of the 1960s and 70s, this work would be recognized as foundational in the making of African literary criticism. During the same decade, Mofokeng submitted an MA thesis on 'A Study of Sesotho Folktales'

Bochabela (Traveller to the East), a Sesotho rendering of John Bunyan's *Pilgrims Progress* and condemned for *Chaka*, his historical novel. See Daniel P. Kunene, *Thomas Mofolo and the Emergence of Written SeSotho Prose* (Johannesburg: Raven Press, 1989), Chapters 4 and 6.

4 A discussion of the cultural project of the New African Movement in South Africa can be found in Ntongela Masilela's *The Cultural Modernity of H.I.E. Dhlomo* (Trenton, NJ: Africa World Press, 2007).

(1951) and a PhD thesis, 'The Development of Leading Figures in Animal Tales in Africa' (1954) to the University of Witwatersrand, considered to be one of the two top universities in South Africa. In spite of its pedigree, Mofokeng's academic work remained unremarked and lost.[5]

How do we explain the neglect or occlusion of Mofokeng from the institution of literary criticism in Africa? One would be tempted to blame it on an old culprit—language politics. After all, as Karin Barber has argued, postcolonial criticism—or the projects that go under that name—have not been interested in texts written in African languages or criticism about them; instead, they have 'promoted a binarized, generalized model of the world which had the effect of eliminating African-language expression from view'.[6] This model has both diminished the place of African languages in the colonial experience while maintaining what Barber calls 'a center-periphery polarity which both exaggerates and simplifies the effects of the colonial imposition of European languages' and turns 'the colonizing countries into unchanging monoliths, and the colonized subject into a homogenized.'[7] Linguistic preferences cannot, however, explain Mofokeng's absence from postcolonial institutions of interpretation. The reason for this is that, in Apartheid South Africa, the use of African languages was closely tied to a state project whose goal was nothing less than the reproduction of the African as a Bantu, the subject of an ethnic enclave—a Bantustan—and hence a

---

5 Ruth Finnegan captures the significance of Mofokeng's work and its absence in her preface to the second edition of her groundbreaking book, *Oral Literature in Africa* (London: Open Book Publishers, 2012): 'I think especially of S. M. Mofokeng's sadly unpublished dissertations [. . .] the inspiration and basis of the linguistic account in my Chapter 3'—p. *xxviii*.
6 Karin Barber, 'African-Language Literature and Postcolonial Criticism', *Research in African Literatures* 26(4) (Winter 1995): 3.
7 Barber, 'African-Language Literature', p. 3.

stranger in the white republic. In order to secure the identity of African groups divided along linguistic lines, the state promoted the use of African languages, but only within the confines of its own projects.[8]

To complicate matters, the Apartheid state allowed the existence of active programmes in African languages at the elite universities of Cape Town and Witwatersrand. Exempted from official racial segregation, these programmes would provide the training ground of a remarkable generation of critics of Africa literature including B. W. Vilakazi (PhD, Witwatersrand, 1945) and A. C. Jordan (PhD, University of Cape Town, 1957). Though lesser known than these towering figures, Mofokeng shared their education and pedigree and he cannot hence be relegated to the rank of a native informant. It is not incidental that Mofokeng was a close associate of C. M. Doke, the topmost scholar of African languages in South Africa or that the *Pelong ya Ka* was published by the University of Witwatersrand Press in 'the Bantu Treasury', a series edited by C. M. Doke and D. T. Cole.[9] However, unlike Vilakazi and Jordan who wrote for the intellectual class, Mofokeng's work was produced in conversation with the untutored. He was an insider/outsider, occupying the space where colonialism and nationalism met and diverged.

---

8 A rich background and context can be found in Nhlanhla P. Maake, 'A Survey of Trends in the Development of African Language Literatures in South Africa: With Specific Reference to Written Southern Sotho Literature *c*.1900–1970s', *African Languages and Cultures* 5(2) (1992): 157–88.

9 This publishing history is discussed in detail by Nhlanhla P. Maake in 'C. M. Doke and the Development of Bantu Literature', *African Studies* 52(2) (1993): 77–88; and Elizabeth Le Roux, 'Black Writers, White Publishers: A Case Study of the Bantu Treasury Series in South Africa', *E-rea* 11(1) (2013). Available at: http://journals.openedition.org/erea/3515 (last accessed on 8 June 2021).

Some biographical and cultural background might help us understand the dialectic of the insider/outsider on the borderlands of South African culture. Eastern Fouriesburg, where Mofokeng was born in 1923 and where he grew up on a farm, is on the border between the Republic of South Africa (more precisely the old Afrikaans-dominated Orange Free State) and the British Protectorate of Basutoland, later the Republic of Lesotho. But this border, like many other lines of division in Southern Africa, was artificial. What it marked was the legal separation of the Sesotho people into two political entities even when they were held together by a common language and culture. Mofokeng could not escape the consequences of this colonial arrangement. Neither could he escape the fact that the road to becoming an intellectual passed through selective colonial institutions such as the Dutch school at Viljoensdrift, where he got his early education, and Adams College, the United Congregationist Church mission school in Natal, where he went for his secondary education. His higher education would start at Fort Hare, the elite black university, where he got his first degree and end at the liberal University of Witwatersrand, where he acquired two advanced degrees in African language literatures. Ordinarily, Mofokeng's career, which included a stint as a teacher at the Bantu High School in Johannesburg and in the Department of African Languages at Witwatersrand, would have consolidated his standing as a member of the elite even under conditions of subjection.

Pelong ya Ka cannot accurately be described as a text produced on the margins. Indeed, Mofokeng's location at the centre of a set of intersecting interests in the culture of late colonialism—the legal-ization and enforcement of the doctrine of racial separation by the state and African cultural assertion as a counterpoint—makes his book an excellent example of the counter-hegemonic work per-formed by texts from elsewhere outside the marginality authorized by the state and its institutions. To put it another way, it was because he was a privileged and well-educated African that Mofokeng's work could go against the grain of the set of desires colonialism sought to bestow on its subjects. Unlike the 'untutored' intellectuals who opened my discussion, Mofokeng did not suffer from the debilitating sense that his education was inadequate.[10] He had all the education available even in the racialized culture of Apartheid. And while his precursors, most notably Thomas Mofolo in *Chaka* and Sol Plaatje in *Mhudi*, saw the recovery of a pre-colonial African past as essential to countering colonial deracination by locating their subjects in history, even when that history was a product of colonial documentation, Mofokeng's work was focused on the mythical or the timeless as a site of African self-fashioning. To be timeless was not to be without a history; rather, it was a claim to perceptual time as the condition of African Being. While Mofolo and Plaatje went out of their way to defend the idea of the African as a subject of history, Mofokeng seemed to have taken the affirmative culture of his Sotho readers for granted and, in the process, reclaimed what Njabulo Ndebele would later call 'the ordinary'.[11]

This concern with the ordinary perhaps helps explain what appears to be the omission, or even repression, of the key historical events surrounding *Pelong ya Ka* or more precisely its moment of production. Mofokeng's book is silent on the cataclysmic events that were shaping and reshaping the Sesotho in the long twentieth

---

10 Without the advantage of a high school or college education, and caught between the educated elite and the manual laborer, Karin Barber notes, this class 'assiduously cultivated literacy without feeling fully entitled to the status with which it was associated.' See 'Introduction: Hidden Innovators in Africa' in *Africa's Hidden Histories: Everyday Literary Making the Self* (Bloomington: Indiana University Press, 2006), p. 5.

11 Njabulo S. Ndebele, 'The Rediscovery of the Ordinary: Some New Writings in South Africa,' *Journal of Southern African Studies* 12(2) (April 1986): 143–57.

century and on the radical reorganization of African lives by the Apartheid regime during those fateful years when the state set out to manage difference through the passage of notorious Apartheid laws such as the Prohibition of Mixed Marriages Act (1949), the Immorality Amendment Act (1950) and the Bantu Education Act (1953). As a teacher and scholar, Mofokeng lived under the shadow of laws that controlled where he could live, work or even teach. Yet *Pelong ya Ka* does not carry the burden of this history.

The question of the Mofokeng's attitude to his time is further complicated by his ambivalent relationship to the cultural formation that enabled his works. *Pelong ya Ka* does not render itself to the project of cultural retrieval promoted by the Paris Evangelical Mission Society at Morija in Lesotho where, beginning in the second half of the nineteenth century, the Sotho were re-imagined under the sign of what came to be known as custom.[12] This does not mean that Mofokeng was not interested in questions of custom as such; but he seemed eager to avoid colonial historiography and its assumption that the Sesotho were nothing more than products of the colonial episteme. What might appear to some readers to be an investment in essentialism—the insistence on an intrinsic Sesotho world—can be read as Mofokeng's counter to the colonial (and Apartheid) state's invention of the Bantu, the African reduced to a figure of the white desire for a manageable other.[13] What Mofokeng

---

12 For the Sesotho or Basuto as they were called in the colonial lexicon, the discourse of custom was firmly established with the publication by the Paris Evangelical Mission of the Reverend D. Fred Ellenberger's *History of the Basuto Ancient and Modern* under the auspices of the colonial government in 1912. An abbreviated Sesotho version, *Histori Ea Basotho* (History of the Basotho) was published at Morija in 1928.

13 Ellenberger's *History of the Basuto* was written at the request of Sir H. C. Sloley, the British Resident Commissioner of Basutoland (now Lesotho). The original manuscript in French was 'written in English' by J. C.

offers is series of meditations, fragments and essays that provide his readers with a conceptual view of the world as what Georg Lukacs called 'sensed experience, as immediate reality, as spontaneous principle of existence . . . an event of the soul, as the motive force of life'.[14]

Pelong ya Ka, translated by Nhlanhla P. Maake as 'In My Heart' is a meditation on the Sesotho worldview outside the categories authorized by colonial knowledge. The first essay in the collection, for example, locates the heart as the center of what it means to be Sotho, 'The Heart Is What the Person Is.' What does it mean to put the heart, rather than the mind, at the centre of being? What makes the heart distinct from soul and mind? Here matters of language and translation open up new vistas. The Sotho word for Heart is *Pelo*, but as we learn from the authoritative *Southern Sotho-English Dictionary*, *pelo* also refers to feelings, emotions, desires, temperament and inner voices. The heart can denote a range of feelings, from happiness to bitterness; it can refer to disparate states of behavior, from kindness to wickedness; it is also connected to language or, more specifically, modes of enunciation or storytelling. *Pelo* is the wide territory inside the person, the fountain of selfhood.[15] In *Pelong ya Ka*, Mofokeng seemed keen to secure the integrity of this inner world. One could even speculate that he ignored the material world, a world defined by racial segregation and a harsh regimen of labour,

---

MacGregor, Assistant Commissioner and colonial ethnographer. The frontispiece in the original edition contained a portrait of Viscount Gladstone, Governor-General and High Commissioner of the Union of South Africa.

14 Georg Lukacs, 'On the Nature and Form of the Essay' in *Soul and Form* (Anna Bostock trans.) (London: Merlin Press, 1974), pp. 1–18.

15 I refer here to the new edition of the *Southern-Sotho English Dictionary*, by A. Mabille and H. Dieterlen, reclassified, revised and enlarged by R. A. Paroz (Morija-Lesotho: Morija Sesuto Book Depot, 1988), pp. 350–1.

because he needed to secure the interior world of the heart as a place where shared experiences and values—loneliness and death, for example—could be privileged as a set of values that were 'universalizable, though never universal'.[16]

What we have here is not a description of practices and processes locked in historical time, nor a discourse on the crisis of a compromised modernity, but a meditation on the process of change as it was experienced by specific agents. Mofokeng understood the process of change and its effects on African life, but he refused to conceive it within the logic of the colonial binary. Consider 'Horse Race,' for example. It starts with memories of a horse race recalled from childhood: 'Once or twice a year in our village, while I was growing up, a big derby used to be held, which was enjoyed by everyone—a horse derby.' This memory is, however, not locked in the past; on the contrary, it is linked to, and compared with, a commercialized horse race in Durban where the beauty of the race is judged according to the fate of a bet:

> They had bet that they were going to win, and how could the race be beautiful if they do not win? When we looked around, we began to see clearly. Here and there you could see those who were excited, here and there you could also see those who were morose. A certain Indian woman even fainted. We started realizing that there is plenty of sadness here.
>
> It took a long time for me to forget that.

Here there is no radical division between the country and the city, between modernity and tradition, or between the past and the present. The differences are laid out in terms of beauty, pleasure and

---

16 See Gayatri Chakravorty Spivak's 'Elsewhere Texts: A General Introduction'.

affect—or their absence. Indeed, Mofokeng would return to the Durban Derby several times hoping that it could rekindle the magic of the Sesotho derby of his childhood, but he would be disappointed by what he found:

> I have gone there several times. Wherever I went I was searching, I thought I would find the joy and excitement of the derby of my childhood: song praises, ululation, real horse racing which is loved by all the Basotho, as it is in their blood as our forefathers used to race, with their cattle. But I found only robbery; I found theft that was permissible; I found joy and sadness, excitement and sorrow. The great joy that is not mixed with sadness, the joy of my childhood, that is no longer here—I cannot find it. It is now many a time that I have asked myself whether the world is getting corrupt. Most times I nearly despair. But now I have found solace that with every person, things do change.

The theme of change runs through these essays, as it always does in South African writing of the period, but this does not lead to the pathological fear of the new supposedly experienced by the African in the city, a pet theme in the writing of white South African writers like Alan Paton. As the narrator transverses a multiplicity of worlds, embracing the nomadic and contingent—chance encounters on trains, idle drives on the highway and the change discovery of the sea, for example—he upends the binaries that have hitherto informed discourse on change in Africa:

> That is how it is, my compatriot. Everywhere things change, there is nothing that stands still, on the same spot. That is how they are created and there is no other way. It was said that we will be born, grow up, grow old and descend into the grave. We will have children and they will also follow that path. It is the way of change.

There are many epiphanies in this book, but the one on boundaries is particularly telling. Having been brought up on the border between South Africa and Lesotho, and having assumed that such boundaries were natural, Mofokeng is surprised to discover that the border between the Republic of South Africa and Swaziland is false:

> In my head I was already imagining a river, and a bridge, and on the other side of the bridge a customs office and next to it a pole wearing a Swaziland flag. While I was imagining these things I suddenly saw 'You are now in Swaziland.' I stopped the vehicle. I looked back, because I thought that I had missed the river. I found nothing; I mean even a neatly woven little fence. I stood there surprised.
>
> No, today I am no longer surprised. I also know why nations keep on fighting, quarrelling over boundaries. It is because of such borders. These things are not even boundaries; they are just a mockery.

Mocking the idea of the border and the institutions that authorized it is one way for Mofokeng to be Sesotho in ways not imagined by the state. Similarly, his constant move between the local and the universal, the centrifugal and centripetal, is an insistence that the Sotho is simultaneously a citizen of two countries and of one world, a world defined by matters of the heart.

The language in which Mofokeng wrote has borne the historical weight of political engineering in South Africa, like the other eight Bantu languages that became officially recognized by the post-apartheid constitution of 1996, and this weight has manifested in how the people who speak it have been named, including the language itself. It is part of the Southern Bantu languages that are spoken in the SADC (Southern African Development Community) region, which comprises Angola, Botswana, Congo (Democratic Republic of Congo), Eswatini, Lesotho, Malawi, Mozambique, United Republic of Tanzania, Zambia and Zimbabwe. These languages transcend political borders but are artificially affiliated to nation states. Sesotho belongs to a cluster of languages that is named Sotho Group, namely, Sepedi or Sesotho sa Lebowa (also Pedi, formerly called Northern Sotho), Sesotho (also Sotho, formerly called Southern Sotho) and Setswana (Tswana, formerly called Eastern Sotho). They are separate languages but as mutually intelligible as Italian, Spanish and Portuguese.

Sesotho is the official language of the Kingdom of Lesotho and one of South Africa's 11 official languages, but, since the early 1960s, South Africa developed a different orthography, a manifestation of the political history of the two countries. In 1910, South Africa became a Union, forged by the descendants of the Dutch and English settlers at the conclusion of the Anglo-Boer War of 1899 to 1903, which is at times given the misnomer of the South African War by certain historians. Lesotho was then known as Basutoland, as it was until independence in 1966.[1] The language in Lesotho has always been referred to as Sesotho, while in South Africa it evolved from being called Southern Sotho to Sotho and eventually Sesotho. From the beginning of the 1950s when apartheid established its draconian and fascist authority through a myriad of segregation laws, the language ramified into two tributaries of literature that were divided not only by the orthographies but also the political landscape. Mofokeng belonged to the South African side of the major dividing landmark, the Caledon River, although in this book Mofokeng imagines artificial borders without natural markers.

Sophonia Machabe Mofokeng (1923–1957) is the first scholar in South Africa to acquire a PhD in Sesotho, a rare qualification among black Africans across disciplines. The degree was conferred by the University of the Witwatersrand, popularly known simply as Wits. He took a position as a Language Instructor in the then Department of Bantu Studies at the alma mater. The designation was politically loaded, because black Africans at that institution could not be afforded the academic title of Lecturer or Professor, which was the privilege of white academics, some of whom had far fewer qualifications that Mofokeng. The act was significant of the institution's tacit capitulation to apartheid laws of the 1950s that excluded black Africans from certain job categories. The status quo reigned supreme despite the institution's image as liberal, and this was evident in its standards of regarding diversity as comprising 'about a

---

1 B. M. Khaketla, *Lesotho 1970: An African Coup Under the Microscope* (London: Christopher Hurst & Co., 1971).

quarter Afrikaans, a quarter Jewish, and the remainder "British" '.[2] Thus, Mofokeng and some of his colleagues, including the renowned Robert Mangaliso Sobukwe, were relegated to a status below their qualifications and calibre.[3] Mofokeng died at the young age of 34, after periodic hospitalizations.[4]

Despite an academic milieu that was not friendly to the advancement of black African scholars and scholarship, Mofokeng wrote three books: a stage play, *Senkatana* (1952), the eponymous protagonist, derived from the legend of 'the swallowing monster' or 'kgodumodumo'; an anthology of essays entitled *Leetong: On Pilgrimage* (1952); and *Pelong ya Ka* (1962),[5] translated from the Sesotho here as *In My Heart*. The fourth work was written in collaboration with Professor Clement Doke, *Textbook of Southern Sotho Grammar* (1957), still the most authoritative and encyclopaedic work on Sesotho grammar.

In reading the primary text, which this translator had read prior to translating and discussed with postgraduate and undergraduate students over several years, one finds nuances of a pervasive melancholic strain in Mofokeng's diction. It is plausible to infer that it connotes a manifestation of autobiographical ambience, reinforced by his fragile state of health and the racially ambivalent academic environment at the University of the Witwatersrand. His meditative tone of voice, drawing on Sesotho wisdom lore (proverbs, maxims,

---

2 Bruce Murray, *Wits 'Open' Years: A History of the University of the Witwatersrand* (Johannesburg: Wits University Press, 1997), p. 166.

3 Nhlanhla P. Maake, 'How Can a Man Die Better: The Life of Robert Sobukwe'. *The Sunday Independent*, 14 September 1997, p. 20.

4 D. J. M. Ngcangca, *Mabalankwe ka Bangodi ba Basotho* (Pietermaritzburg: Shuter & Shooter, 1989).

5 Nhlanhla P. Maake, 'Mofokeng, Sophonia Machabe' in Simon Gikandi (ed.) *Encyclopedia of African Literature* (New York: Routledge, Taylor and Francis, 2003), p. 340.

idioms, folklore, customs, and traditions), symbolism and figurative style, pose challenges that feel like a defiance and resistance of the primary text to be reduced to a secondary text. The morphological, semantic and syntactic differences between varieties of Sesotho remain in spite of their convergence and intercourse through colonialism and coloniality. And, as Gikandi points out, Mofokeng attempts to write from a mindset insusceptible to these binary oppositions. Such extratextual elements contributed to confounding the translator.

As a postgraduate student of history, the debates on choice of language between English and local languages, which ensued in the period that preceded his decade of writing, would not by any means have been lost to him. The autobiographical, historical and political signs of the time are not manifest in the surface structure of the text but tend to mark their existence in the deep structure. It is these subtle and paradoxical complexities that rendered translation of this text an exercise in negotiating a truce.

I had to take a dual approach: first, negotiate the territorial space between Mofokeng's variety[6] of Sesotho and contemporary varieties, then invite it to the English idiom. Let me address only a few layers of this complexity, namely, gender neutrality of Sesotho pronouns, non-equivalence, one-to-one and one-to-many equivalence, proverbs and idiomatic expressions and symbolism, interjective expressions, narrative technique of familiarity and intimacy, humour and pathos.

In Sesotho and other Bantu languages, there is no gender denotation in the third person pronouns, 'he', 'she' and 'they/them' and inanimate pronouns 'it' and 'they/them'. In the former instance, reference to indefinite personae called for choices to discriminate, or adopt the plural third-person pronoun, 'they/them', which in

---

6 I am using this neutral term in lieu of 'dialect', which is loaded with negative connotations.

most instances sounded clumsy, and had to be rehabilitated by circumventing this ubiquitous pronoun. In the former and latter instances, English denotes third-person personal pronouns and inanimate pronouns with three and two lexical items respectively, whereas in Sesotho the pronoun is dictated by noun prefixes that denote singularity or plurality, and there are 14 such noun prefixes. Reducing them to the limited versions of English turned out to be a task that called for stressful and frustrating paradigmatic and syntagmatic choices and constriction.

The essay entitled 'Botho', translated as 'Character' was one of the most daunting texts. This word appeared with such high frequency that it seemed to taunt and dare the translator. The author used it to mean a variety of English equivalents, i.e. 'personality', 'character', 'humanity' and 'humaneness', and in certain instances Mofokeng alludes to all of these in one lexical item. Gikandi refers to 'heart' as a multivalent word.

Proverbs and idioms were compressed and literalized more than they should have been. The Sesotho narrative technique of direct reference to the addressee by using endearment terms or second-person reference, which Mofokeng uses abundantly, have been buttressed by footnotes.

Humour and pathos are some of the most difficult aspects to translate, I suppose in any language. As stated earlier, Mofokeng's diction is predominantly melancholic, to an extent that lightning flashes of humour are overshadowed by the general tone of his voice. It is this aspect that I approached with intense apprehension, if not trepidation. Whether the reader of this text will find them should perhaps be regarded as a matter of either the reader's poetic sensitivity or susceptibility (I am saying this *sotto voce*), but more so the translator's success (or otherwise) in carrying over both the lightness of the author's humour and the weight of his pathos. The challenge of pathos became a matter of more than just transference from the source text to the target text, but it vexed me even within the language of the former, not to mention the latter. In order to capture it, I felt a strong inclination to using words of Latinate instead of Anglo-Saxon etymology, as in the essays, 'Bodutu' and 'Lenyalo', which passively resisted translation as 'Loneliness' and 'Marriage' respectively but seemed to prefer 'Solitude' and 'Matrimony.' Throughout the translation of these essays, and others, I found this dilemma persistent. What eventually held sway was the conviction to submit to Mofokeng's leaning towards a conversational style, which coexists with a formal undertone.

Creating and maintaining a balance between the reluctance of Sesotho to meet English and the reluctance of English to welcome and accommodate Sesotho is the nightmare that I think every translator might have suffered. I took solace in their spiritual company. The third dimension of the problem was the burden of one's European bi-culturalism that Gayatri Chakravorty Spivak refers to in her General Introduction. It subconsciously tampered with attempts to flex my imagination sufficiently, as Simon Gikandi put it in his Introduction, to transcend programming of assuming cultural markers.

Different versions of Sesotho at times refused to accommodate each other. What was tormenting in this mission was Mofokeng's haunting shadow over my English rendition, in what felt like his act of exorcism, to prevent this translation from trampling on his heart, mind or soul, his pelo pondering the themes of his essays. Another dimension came from the fact that I once served in the academic institution and department in which Mofokeng served, albeit about three decades after him in the early 1980s and late 90s, professing in the same discipline. By that time, racial attitudes had somewhat changed from the overt to the covert. Perhaps the most grievous fault on my part was that I felt the responsibility of reincarnating Mofokeng in another language which he had mastered far better than I ever will. I was also confounded by the multivocality of the various Englishes that inhabit the postmodern globe.[7]

I put the book away for a while. And then, Professor Spivak and Dr Maithufi, two esteemed colleagues, discussed the early drafts of my translation with me. At times their suggestions struck a chord that was in harmony with a dormant note in my mind, at others we agreed to disagree. But generally, the translation was enriched by their input, observations, comments and suggestions. I also wish to extend my gratitude to Seagull Books editor, Sunandini Banerjee, for her sharp eye that ironed out stylistic infelicities. She listened to the idiom of the original text and her editorial suggestions enriched the final version of the book. I beg the readers, with my open palm on my heart, not to attribute any deficiency that they may find in this translation to the three colleagues who were my companions on this journey, but rather to my intransigence or failure to fully hear the orchestra of Mofokeng's style and to conduct it harmoniously in another language, despite attentive listening. I thought I heard Mofokeng, but perhaps the fault lay in that I did not do so with my ears, but with my eyes as I translated from the written page instead of interpreting from the *tessitura* of his voice. It might have even been better to listen to Mofokeng's voice as it resonated, not in my mind but in my heart.

January 2020

---

7 Gloria Anzaldúa, 'How to Tame a Wild Tongue' in Donald McQuade and Robert Atwan (eds), *The Writer's Presence: A Pool of Readings* (Boston: Bedford/St Martin's, 2000), pp. 311–21.

In My Heart

THE HEART

The heart is such an important organ in a person's body that a person cannot live without it. We know by its beating that a person is still alive. When it beats slowly, we also know that life is no longer resilient, that the lights are about to be switched off. Whereas when it has come to a standstill, we know that the days are gone. It is an organ that is absolutely indispensible in the body, but difficult to treat. In most cases, when doctors say that a person has a cardiac ailment, we tend to live in apprehension that that one has already left us for the hereafter.

The beating of the heart does not only betoken that a person is still alive—it can also tell us many other things. Sometimes the heart tells us when a person is frightened. You will find it beating such that it seems that it will break through the ribs. It is not just that; when a thief is hiding safely, people not seeing him, perhaps having given up on catching him, they see him suddenly emerging, and running away, the reason being that he heard his heart beating so hard that he believed everyone else heard it too!

The heart is powerful. That is why we Basotho talk about it so much. When a person is eating, and the food does not go down well, when he feels nauseous, he says: 'This food does not go down well. It is sitting on my heart,' or 'My heart is bilious.' Perhaps a glutton is sitting next to us, a person who is never satiated, who keeps eating greedily, eating with his eyes wide open as if food will run away. We steal a glance at one another, and when he turns around the corner, one of us says: 'Hey people! what a big heart he has, *banna!*'[1]

Even in revelry, when we are happy, we keep on talking about it, not least in sorrow. How can it not rear its head in such conversation, for joy and sorrow are two sides of the coin of our lives? Something has happened which makes you happy, and you say that it has whitened your heart, it has cleansed it and it is pure. Ah, a clean thing is like snow, it is pure white.

You are content, you are happy, your heart is clean; you are now white-hearted. Perhaps you are disappointed, you feel very sad, you, that is, you and your heart, because you are one and the same thing. Then we say you are broken-hearted. You are in sorrow like when a person who is bereaved, who is in darkness, blackness. And your heart (that is, you) is black; it is in darkness, in sorrow. Or something disappoints you, and you feel as if your heart is sinking deep down inside you, as if there is a heavy burden that makes your emotions sink. In explaining your condition, you say: 'I am despondent in my heart.'

We have already said that the heart and the person are one and the same thing. The heart is what the person is. It is therefore not surprising that we describe a person's character by his heart. We talk about people who have good hearts, that is, edible hearts. I think that if it were edible, we would find a kind person's heart delectable, like a person's features. When it comes to patience and kindness and goodness, we regard them as signs that the heart of the possessor is

---

1 This is an exclamation of wonder or surprise or shock, equivalent to 'Oh man!' or 'Oh my God!' It is used by male persons. Literally it means 'men!', and is equivalent to 'basadi!' (Women!), which is used by female persons.

present—a person with a heart—that is, an immense one; or a long one, or a soft one, so much that you can do anything that you like without breaking it! Whereas when you are bereft of patience, it is understood that your heart is short, small, this little, it may run out, and you say: 'I have run out of heart!' Perhaps you are wise, have advices because your head is functioning; in Sesotho, we are not bothered about that head, even though it is actually the head that functions. We simply say: 'What a wise-hearted person,' or 'what a soft-hearted person,' when you are sympathetic; or 'What a hard-hearted person,' when you are cruel.

In Sesotho, your heart is what matters most, not your physical features. Your physical features are not what you are—what you are is what is inside you, that is, where your heart is, where we don't see. What you are is what is manifested in your acts. Your heart is right inside you, it represents what is inside you; it is your humanity, your being. When a person says: 'I give you my heart,' that means he or she gives you his or her inner self, he or she gives himself or herself to you completely. Your heart is your inner being.

We speak in the same vein when a person dillydallies. We hit the nail on the head when we say that you have two hearts, which means that you are divided in two. And this is a very painful thing indeed, which enervates a person, which makes him or her weak. Be patient with me, my friends, for I am in a dilemma now. One heart says I must keep quiet, lest I provoke people while they are relaxed, and waste their time with so much ado about nothing, lest they start swearing at me and by doing that cause me sorrow. Another says I must narrate what is here IN MY HEART, and relieve it of its baggage, so that it not sink but be at peace; maybe when I am done, I will be white-hearted. I will nonetheless narrate, but be long-hearted please!

CHARACTER

A person's character is hidden, even though it is something that we would like to know. We want to know it because if we know it, we know how to work with the person in tranquillity. If we knew it, we would know that such-and-such a person is a crook, or so-and-so is a thief, even before they do something offensive to us. We would understand each other and many quarrels would be avoided. This means that we would have no quarrels in families, fighting in villages and wars among nations. And that is another matter.

Have you ever felt how wonderful it is when someone narrates news, telling how she was in fear because of not knowing what the person who owns what she has spoilt will say? Or one would say: 'I was deceiving her, and I touched a wrong button on that fateful day. I saw dust,' or 'Matlakala[1] has indeed been bewitched. There is no other way. Do you think that you can work with a person for years and years, lending each other belongings, or just taking possession even when the owner is not present, and then today she bursts just like that, and goes to the extent of beating you with a stick because you took her spade in her absence while you have been taking his plough? This is witchcraft.'

---

1 A female name.

Such things do happen. It is painful when they happen. It is good when they are narrated. They are painful, but they are good and they make life exciting because they spice it. Without them, life would be a bland thing, without spice, just too sweet. But if a person's character were a visible thing, which could be seen by everyone, such things would not happen. Who would dare stir a hornet's nest knowing that is what he is doing? A hornets' nest is disturbed by mistake; it is disturbed only when one does not know that it is there in the grass. A person gets into trouble by happenstance. When you know that there is a ghost at the cemetery at 10 at night, you don't just pass by; you only pass by when it is a must. Perhaps you try to go round about, and end up falling into ditches out there in the wilderness, and then people say that you were led astray by a ghost, or you were attracted by a mythical monster. Yes, if a person's character were visible, matters would be totally different from how they are today. We would be like machines.

A machine, a car, a train, a ship or an aeroplane—all of them are similar. A car moves when there is still fuel in it and it is in good shape, we know well that when it takes off, you press there, do this and that and you will hear it roar. And when you also tread there and there, pulling here and there, you will feel it starting to move slowly (that is, if you know how to drive), or jumping like a horse (that is, if you do not know how to drive). When you touch here and there again, it stops, switches off. When you touch any button, you already know what it will do. You don't even think. Other machines are also like that, the train is similar, ships are like that and aeroplanes are like that. But we people are not like that, and it is good that we are not like that. Our personality is something hidden, which is not visible that our eyes can see it as they can see the beauty or ugliness on a person's face.

But even when it is hidden like that, we search for it. Tumelo[2] wants to understand Tebelo so that he can work with her harmoniously. That is also Tebelo's[3] wish. Each and every one of us rejoices when one finds a person that one understands, and whose personality is almost transparent. Such people we also like, even when his personality tells us that he is a crook. You will hear someone saying: 'I like Tshepo[4] even though he is a thief. He does not hide his kleptomania, he does not pretend to be a trustworthy person. He is a thief and he does not hide it. He has a one-sided character.' That is why we derive pleasure when we read a storybook, because in its pages we find people whose personality we know completely. They are the creatures of the writer, and he or she gives us pleasure by telling us everything about them. We end up feeling that we know them even better than our friends. Their character is exposed. How pleasant it is to expose it!

We try by all means to expose a person's character, and also to know that there are many ways of exposing that personality.

Every person's deeds come from his or her feelings, they come from his or her heart. We do not know what is in the depth of his or her feelings, we cannot see it, but we know and also see the works and deeds that are born from that depth. We are thus able to read what is in the deep by observing what comes from there. We say that a charitable deed cannot be born in a place that stinks with hatred and bad spirit, as a white sheet of paper like this one, will never come from mud. Therefore when we see such a deed, we know that it comes from a good spirit. That deed gives us an opportunity to peep through just a small hole, to see what is inside the depth of a person's feelings.

---

2 A male name.
3 A female name.
4 A male name.

But if we were to wait for such deeds without having got used to a person, we would only know each other well when we have grey hair, when we are approaching seventy years of age, which we have been given here on earth. What would you think of a young man who has seen a young woman, feeling that he loves her but having to wait until her deeds reveal what is in her inner feelings? Such would marry at a very ripe age. Even then, at the time when he gets married, he might discover that the deeds of his beloved did not come from her feelings, that she did only what she did because she wanted to please him. Such deeds do not spring forth from her character. They are deceitful.

We are sojourners in this world, but we love it. We are sorry that we do not have enough time to live in it, this world that has been created for us by the Creator of all. As deeds take a long time and may deceive us, we have other ways in which we can learn how to read other people's personalities. We start by reading a person's face. And that is just because when we think of people we think of their faces. When we see a person with her back towards us, we are unable to tell whether she is Morongwe or Morongwenyana[5]. When she is facing us and the body is hidden, that is, even if she shows only her face through a window, we easily get to know her. Faces are what distinguish people. Each and every one of us has hers, hers alone, no matter how similar we can be. It is for this reasons that we tend to think that the character of a person is written on her face.

Those who know say that a forehead also speaks. When it is plain, it signifies that a person is kind. When it has wrinkles or has a vertical line between the eyes, oh! it signifies abundance of intelligence.

Some say that when a forehead is like this and that, it signifies intelligence because it wrinkles up like that when a person is pondering over difficult things. When you go down and get to the eyes:

5 Female names.

'Oh, eyes full of kindness and love, soft eyes!' 'Hey People! so-and-so, you say that that person is your friend? I am scared of his eyes. They are full of trickery. Why does he shy away from looking at people in the eye? Another: 'Hey, a man with such red eyes as his has been a serial killer for long!' 'Man, what a fierce person! When he merely looks at you, you feel like vanishing!' As for this last-mentioned kind of eye, if you have not seen it, just take a deliberate visit to a police station, or ask young men who are wooing whether they have not seen a young maiden's father looking at them like that!

The nose is also significant. It can make a person ugly even when he is quiet; you find it sulky, as if the person is fierce, with an evil heart making him fierce like a bulldog. Some noses signify outright vanity. A human being is also like that. A mouth that signifies mischief is that of a person who is always pouting it so that it eventually looks like a chunk of meat, whereas a person who is used to smiling is quite transparent. They say that the chin also counts, but I don't know how it can be conspicuous in the case of a person who is perpetually concealing it under a bush of beard!

It is not only the face that exposes a person to us; even the voice. Some think that it is the sound of a person's voice that reveals her or his personality. But I do not believe that it is so. It is not the voice that reveals a speaker's character but the manner in which she or he speaks, the way words are enunciated. Because two people whose voices are so similar that you cannot distinguish between them when singing can still have different styles of speaking, and that difference is caused by the manner in which they articulate their sentences.

But all these are things that are seen on the face or appear there. As for the voice, or the manner of speaking, we also take it that it comes from the face because it comes out of the mouth. But there is something else which can reveal a person's character. I mean footsteps.

Footsteps signify many things. There are footsteps of a fat person, an obese person; of a person who is as thin as a twig, of a very thin person, of a fierce person, of a person who is diligent or a lazy one; of a confident person or one as brave as a soldier, of a cowardly one or a shy one, one who skulks like a dog going to steal bones. There are footsteps of a person who is weak, who is ailing, who is limping; and there are those of a strong one, who is healthy. Footsteps also symbolize their owners. We often hear a person saying: 'Who is that one walking like Moferefere?'[6] Saying that just because he heard only footsteps. Footsteps and a person go together. There is no person who walks without making footsteps, and there are no footsteps that can be heard without a person walking.

I tell you that even this conscience of ours that is strong, that judges us when we commit sins, that does not give us rest until we dump them, that guards us every day, it also seems to have footsteps because it seems as if it is always following us. When you are sitting quietly, and there is something wrong that you have done, or when you have problems, when your heart is beating, it usually seems like the footsteps of an indefatigable person, a person whose footsteps are always the same night and day, a person who is following us wherever we go even when we wish to escape from her or him, a person who has patience, a person who is with us till death do us part. It usually seems as if . . . no, not that it usually seems as if, it is actually that way. Our hearts beat with the footsteps of The Good Shepherd, of 'The Hound of Heaven',[7] and the day the heart stops is the day that the Shepherd finds his lost sheep out of the nine hundred and ninety-nine, his truant sheep which has wandered, and He picks it up with joy and says: 'Rise up, hold my hand, and follow me.'

----

6 A male name.
7 Francis Thompson, 'The Hound of Heaven' (1893).

LONELINESS

It was winter during the month of May, that is, when it started to be very cold. I had woken up in the morning, that very same day, which was a day for resting, one of these days which our children call a holiday. I was prepared to go and visit my friend in Thwathwa Township.[1] When I got into the train I nearly leapt for joy for I bumped into Diphapang, one of the boys that I'd grown up with. I jumped because no one knew where he was. He was an apostate.

'Hey man, miracles will never cease indeed! I was already dying with the loneliness of travelling alone, then it was driven away by you, of all people?'

'There we are, there it is, my dear friend. You have really matured! Look at your little beard! Truly *Mme*[2] Mmadi Phapang will really be surprised the day she sees you. Hey man, do you ever make an appearance, appe . . . !'

'Why should I do that? Not me. I swore that "never," the day I left, the last I visited that place.'

---

1 A ghetto in the east of Johannesburg.
2 The word literally means 'mother', but can also refer to an elderly woman or be used as an endearment term for any female person irrespective of her age.

'What a cruel child! Dihoro hastened to describe you that way, before he even understood you well. Why did you make that oath?'

'Do you think it's good when you have two weeks of holidays, when instead of resting you suffer because of loneliness?'

We laughed, chatted pleasantly, reminisced about old times when we were still little boys. Time passed swiftly, and the train nearly passed my station, with me.

'Go well, Diphapang. Don't hide yourself, man.'

'Oh, now you leave me with such loneliness. Stay well, home boy!'

The train pulled away and moved on. It seems there was no one at home where I was going.

My friend was awoken when he heard me reprimanding his dog which was about to cause damage to my Sunday pants. When I asked him why he was sleeping during the day, he told me that as he was left alone at home, he was afraid that he might be lonely. I started wondering and thinking about loneliness.

*

A person is ill, he does not want to lie down, does not want to remain at home when people have gone to work. The Basotho say that when a person is down with illness, she or he tends to feel extremely alone. There is truth in that, as in many things among the Basotho. A person who is down with illness is usually left behind alone. He suffers from loneliness. In his loneliness, he has time to feel the pains that would not reach his heart had he been with other people. He feels lost, forsaken. He realizes that he is not allowed to go to work with other people, to go where they go, because he is ill. It is understandable that illness is a powerful thing. Where could it be? Ouch! It is a little pain there . . . oh, another one this side; the neck is tired, it is painful. Hmm, he is ill indeed.

But when people come back! When people arrive, loneliness vanishes; they chat, and they laugh.

The sick person laughs such that the mouth is so wide open that the molars are exposed (one with a hole). Pains are gone. Is it that he has been in real pain or suffering from loneliness? Loneliness really does kill.

Another one is ill. This one is sick to death's door, or as they say, it is a matter of life and death. The voice is already weak, the pupils are now white and the eyes seem to be heavy. The neck is like a little twig. Even when she or he laughs, the effort is heavy work. She or he no longer wants to speak. When people come to her or him, and try to chat, all she or he answers is 'yes' and 'no'. Even when they look at her or him, she or he is shy. She or he likes to lie down alone, gazing at the ceiling, or her or his hands, fidgeting with the wool of the blanket. She or he likes to be alone, right in that loneliness where others complain about suffering from loneliness.

What is it that healthy people are scared of, even those who are only a little sick? What is it that attracts people who are seriously ill, who are sick in body and soul? Yes, because even those who are sick in spirit do not want to be disturbed, they want to be left alone, they like the loneliness, the wilderness!

The wilderness is where real strength is found because that is where we are able to examine ourselves, to introspect, to look at our footsteps, to inspect our ways thoroughly, to see our weaknesses, to see where we strayed from the path, to see where we caused problems for ourselves even though we usually think they were caused by other people. The wilderness is where we are able to examine our consciences; we are able to hear them clearly because we are near our Creator. When we return, we come back strong, because we know our weaknesses and our mistakes. We come back having weathered the storms that were in our hearts. We come back with peace in our hearts. And we find peace in abundance amid the crowds that we were shunning. We find that there is peace in the world if only it is present in our hearts. The world is a mirror, and in it we see what is in us. If there is chaos in you, it is also just as chaotic. If there is no peace in you, there is likewise no peace in it. Real peace is that which is in a person's heart. She or he will never find it if she or he does not know loneliness. It is a great gift of loneliness.

*

You still say: 'I am suffering from loneliness!' Why don't you just say: 'I am suffering from noise?'

DEATH

A certain man was riding a bicycle and behind him came a motor-car. When he was asked, he said he did not know how it actually happened. But in the wink of an eye he found himself on the ground. He rose suddenly, and crawled to the side of road. As he was crawling, there was a screeching of motorcar tyres behind him. It just squashed his poor bicycle, such that he could also have died had he not crawled, unlike those who, after hitting the ground, try to find their bearings a bit.

When he survived this mishap, there were many people who were walking by the roadside, but the one who surprised many is a little grandchild of Eve[1] who only said:

'Hey people! this person has saved himself for another kind of death!'

All and sundry kept exclaiming:

'That woman is a witch!' 'She doesn't know what she is talking about! She is talking nonsense!' Another one: 'She needs a whip. If we were not in urban areas I would have been on her already!' Another one: 'You are just pretending to be surprised. That is their way, that's how women are.'

---

1 Female person.

Indeed, it is true. When the progeny of Eve knows the truth, she tells it without qualms, irrespective of whether she will offend other people, like a child. That one knew that death was a curse (if it is indeed), our curse, and there is no way that we can survive it. When we evade this one, we spare ourselves for the next one, etcetera. She was telling only the truth, but telling it the Eve way.

*

The bell is ringing. It is not ringing as usual when it calls us to prayer or service. It rings, and goes quiet; it rings, and goes quiet. When it rings this way, it quietens noise everywhere in the village. Even the boys who were kicking a ball stop. They are not stopping because there is a funeral, but because they know that if someone sees them, they will be thrashed at home in the evening or at school the next day. It is quiet all over the little village. Women appear in the streets wearing their black clothes, or red or white ones or green ones, etcetera, according to their denominations. They are holding handkerchiefs in their hands. They are not talking; they are going where the deceased is lying. When they get there, they sit down. There in front, near the coffin, one can hear the tiny voice of someone who is weeping. All eyes go there. Oh, poor child! The Reverend is now speaking, ' . . . may the congregation come forth to see our sibling for the last time . . . for the last time . . . we will keep on singing.'

'Oh! What is life to us?' The congregation takes up that hymn. They ask themselves. And one by one they come to give a glance at what had happened. They find their sibling lying still, handsome, as if he will rise and say: 'Yes, servant of God,' as he was wont to greet people when he was alive. But he is silent, eternally silent. Yesterday, last week, in the month gone by, yesteryear, he was talking, laughing with them joyfully, without knowing that he would be silent thus. But there it is, there it is now. But what is this? What is living to us? It is just mist.

The hammer is tolling now. The last nails are being hit. He is locked in there now, alone, not stirring, not breathing. The light of the sun he will never see again, cool air, rains, snow, frost; he is eternal darkness until . . . yes, until when? Who knows? Perhaps those who have come to the funeral are thinking this because they start weeping. Lovers have parted, orphans are left behind. There they take her, they go out of the village with him, the song pervading the place as they walk that way towards the little valley outside the village. 'My days are flowing.' They have now crossed the little valley. They are now heading to the cemetery where they have prepared a small edifice for her.

The burial service comes to an end now. 'Dust to dust, ashes to ashes . . .' that is the Reverend who is uttering those heavy words. The congregation ask themselves: 'Is it that we are dust, we are ashes?' They are sprinkling dust, and while they are sprinkling it the hymn is still going into crescendo '. . . those who were helping me are gone . . .' The wailing of sorrow rises again. The widow does not want to rise, to go back home . . . or is she weak?

Death is cruel. They all concurred, that it is cruel.

*

There are white sheets. Beds stand in a neat row. Wherever you look this word, neatness, is emblazoned, I mean, even when you breathe it seems as if you breathe in this neatness. On every bed lies a patient. In this corner lies Sera. It is not the first time that she has come to this hospital. Every year she spends two or three months here. When you look at her, you might think that she will be healed and be healthy. You still have hope, but she is sick of the daily journey to this place. She already knows that even if she recuperates today, next year she will come back again, or this very same year at Christmas time. Today it seems she is in a bad state. There she is, calling a nurse. Let us also come closer.

'Nurse, I am dizzy, I can't see clearly. Please help!'

The nurse raises her eyes. She looks at the documents at the head of the bed. She sees the thermometer line that shows that her temperature is 104°. She already knows that temperature is the cause of her dizziness. But she does not talk. She simply says:

'Sleep, and try to rest, *ntate*,[2] it will be over just now!' There goes the nurse. Molahlehi writhes, he turns over; his pain starts again, rises, he cannot hear properly. Now he only groans: 'm . . . m . . . mmmm . . . '

'Nurse, nurse!'

'What's the matter *ntate*?'

'Oh, my child, call the doctor please!'

The doctor arrives. He checks, he touches here and there. He is confused. He does not know what to do in order to eliminate the pain that Sera is suffering from. He has reached the stage where his knowledge ends. He simply gives her words of courage. He goes away. Sera is left alone, alone in her pains, like a person alone in the desert or in the middle of the sea.

'Help me please, help me please!' Where will she get help, when even a doctor has surrendered? She no longer thinks clearly, she does not hear properly! She is piteous. Her face twists into a grimace, she throws her arms this way and that way, she moves her head from side to side.

Minutes are ticking, they have now secluded her from other patients with a curtain. She can no longer see, even though she is staring with dilated eyes.

---

2 Lliterally 'father', but also generally used to refer to a person old enough to be the speaker's father. Sometimes, it may also be used to mean 'husband', 'mister' and / or 'sir'.

'God, help me, Father . . . end my pains!' Minutes are ticking. The pain cuts deep, it is still audible. Eventually it subsides; it becomes quiet, she is now departing. God has answered her prayer. The little one is gone . . .

Death . . . is death cruel indeed?

*

We all lose patience when something does not come to an end. We desire change. Even when something is extremely pleasant, we do not want it to be a daily routine. It is well that we lose patience. All things have a beginning and end. Including our lives. But when our end comes, we cry, especially we who remain behind. It is not Sera who is weeping but her relatives. As far as Sera is concerned death is not painful, it is painful to us. Why?

Death is a messenger, the emissary of the Lord. How can a messenger be at fault? He is sent to call us back whence we came, to the light in which we believe. Or do we really believe? Perhaps we do not believe fully, it is for this reason that we have doubt about the next home. The world has conquered us; we do not want to part with it. When the time comes, when this necessary end comes, we are scared, we shiver, we say: 'Death is cruel.' But what is the use? Because we have to meet it, even though we do not like to. It is the curse that Eve brought upon us.

*

'Hey people! this poor person has saved himself for another death,' so says the progeny of Eve.

HORSE RACING

Once or twice a year in our village, while I was growing up, a big derby used to be held, which was enjoyed by everyone—a horse derby. When we read the notice about its date, we would not forget, we would hanker for it. Not only us, because girls and women and men used to attend it, because it was one of the very few festivals that could bring together boys, women and men. Oops! I nearly forgot ... and young men and maidens. Men who came from rural areas used to abduct maidens at the derby. It was a big day, and only old people and very little children stayed behind at home.

Notices would announce that prices included pants, light blankets, skirts, *matlama* blankets and also a little money. As for the horses, they were ridden only by boys, some of them rode wearing loin skins, especially those from rural areas. But these loin cloths did not disadvantage them from beating those who were wearing pants. Most of the horses were not even bridled, and when the boys rode them you would see their legs just hanging, especially when they were riding emaciated horses, because they were not even lined up in order, let alone in terms of age. Some of them were ridden from where they came. This happened because their owners were not prepared to take part in the derby, but when they saw crossbreeds that were going to race, you could hear a person saying: 'No, if these are going to run, this one of mine can also go.' As a result, they just ran in a mix, crossbreeds and pedigree horses. But you would love them, you too, when you saw them shooting away from their starting point. They were a crowd, a whirlwind of dust. You would also see that they were racing neck–and neck, each to be first at the post. The men who were sitting near the finishing line whistled. Someone jumped and said: '*There we go*! Everyone for himself and the devil takes the hindmost!' If you can't run, you better give up!' When he said that, it was as if he had said to the women: 'Go!' and they started ululating and the men could feel their blood boiling. At that moment you would see the boys who were riding doing wonders on the horses, especially the one in the lead. He was not riding but kneeling on it, whipping it this side and that side, head down, all you could see was the loin skin. Maybe two will reach the post parallel. Then they would break into an argument:

'You didn't beat me, man!'

'I beat you hands down!'

'Do you think that that crossbreed of yours can beat this pedigree?'

'Which one is a crossbreed? Do you hear that you a swearing at me, man?'

If a horse and its owner are one and the same, matters are now in a bad state. Maybe the argument will end thus:

'We can start all over again.' Indeed, they go back to start, to end that argument once and for all.

Particular people keep certain matters alive. They exist while they are still there. But the day they migrate or pass on, they all disappear. Thus, it was in our village.

*

There is a famous city here in the Republic of South Africa. But there is a time of the year when it is the only one that is spoken about. It is in winter, during the months of June and July, mostly towards the end of June and the beginning of July. I am talking about the city of Durban. Reasons? Simply because there is the biggest derby in this Republic held there, the one called 'July Handicap'.

At some point, we stayed behind in that city after school went into recess. We were scared of the winter over there, beyond the Vaal River or the Caledon or Lesotho. There were quite a number of us. Towards the end of June, we started seeing the city of Durban changing. We saw when people arrived, throngs, people who came from afar, most of them speaking Sesotho. Some accompanied their white employers who came for the holidays, which meant that they made it a point that their holidays coincided with this derby. Others came of their own accord, just for this derby.

Everywhere in the city, when that day came close, there was no conversation except for: 'Which one is going to win?' Wherever you went, at a shop or restaurant, in the train or bus; or when you spoke to the rickshaw or a white person or an Indian or whoever, that was the question. Wherever you went, everyone would give you the name of the horse which he thought was going to win, even when you did not ask, because as far as they were concerned it made no sense that you would be in that city at that time and not be interested in hearing anything about the derby. The question is: 'Do you want money?' Who would not want it? 'If you want money, go and bet such-and-such.' Eventually you would see that, according to their narrative, all the eleven or so horses would win, that is, they would all run like machines. Indeed, when you saw them in the photos, you could see that was possible.

When that day arrived, we found that there were no people anwhere in that city, as if they had all emigrated. We also went there to see this great wonder. We found multitudes of people, and arguments in abundance. The time struck, and we saw the race horses; we saw them going to the starting line of the race course; when the gates opened, we saw a marvellous thing, and I believed that indeed it was possible that they could all win. They galloped formed like a wall, without anyone in the lead, without anyone trailing. They held on that way until they came closer to the crowd. Anxiety set in. The boys pulled out their sticks, simultaneously, as if they were given the command by one person; they started whipping them, whipping and really pushing. Oh, when they passed next to us, they passed, they passed in great speed but now they were no longer in line.

My friends and I marvelled and said, what a beautiful race. And that was true. That nearly provoked people to pounce on us! One of them told us that we are talking just . . . 'How can it be a beautiful race when they did not start properly, because 9 did not start off at the same time with the others.' 'No, 9 started off well, it's 11 that did not start off properly!' They had bet that they were going to win, and how could the race be beautiful if they did not win? When we looked around, we began to see clearly. Here and there you could see those who were excited, here and there you could also see those who were morose. A certain Indian woman even fainted. We started realizing that there is plenty of sadness here.

It took a long time for me to forget that.

*

Years have passed and I have forgotten that day. Today I am in another big city. There is also a derby here but it is not a once-in-a-while affair, but a daily one. I have been there and I have seen it.

There I found that horses were arranged neatly according to their races. The one that beats others is burdened with a heavy load.

If it continues to lead, the load is increased. At times, it is taken out of that race and moved up to a higher league. Horses there do wonders. They are different from those that I knew in my childhood, except for the fact that they have four legs. At times, a certain horse is known as a crossbreed that never wins a race. But on another day it leads them way ahead, to an extent that they seem as if they are not running but standing still. From that day people took note of it, and started putting their bets on it. But it got wind of that, and went back to its bad performance again. When they have forgotten about it again, it takes them by surprise and they see it leading again. Witch of a horse! Or the fault lies with its jockey?

Here they are not ridden by boys who sit astride them wearing loin skins. Today it is men. When they are far out there you can swear that they are boys, but when they come closer you can recognize by their cheeks and eyes that they are men, riding tightly close to each other. Do not undermine them, because those who know them say that they have wives and children. As for cars, they drive posh ones! Fire. (I wonder how some of them can reach the car brakes, because of how very tall they are!) When one takes a walk with his wife, it seems he is in the company of his mother. Those who know (for there are quite many of them here) say that some of these manikins are big farmers, and others are attorneys who have deserted legal practice. That is how money is. They are not simply riding but they are working for their children. If you see a horse seeming to sniff, do not be taken by surprise, do not be taken aback because it is not just doing so, but there is a *thokolosi*[3] riding it. And also remember that it has its handler. Their handlers are visible, dear friend. Moreover, when you get there you do not even have to look for them, because they look like one of

---

3 A mythical dwarf-like water sprite, kept by and sent on mischievous errands by a witch or evil person. Also referred to as *tikoloshe*.

Moshoeshoe's great grandchildren who was loved dearly by the Basotho. They do not smoke these small cigarettes, they are too small for them; they smoke big ones that befit their bodies, which are rolled up, called cigars. Those are owners of the horses. They can smell the direction from which the wind will be blowing when a crossbreed horse changes into a thoroughbred horse. They bet in hundreds and hundreds; they live by taking yours and mine, that is, those of us who do not know how to tell a crossbreed horse from others. No wonder, they are known and are followed by people who are in haste to receive the crumbs that fall from the rich man's table, the idea being to cock their ears and hear which horse so-and-so has put his bet on. No, dear friend, these horse owners are totally different from the horse owners that I knew in my childhood. Those raced seriously, they raced with all their souls; that is why they sang their praises. They were racing more for victory than the prize.

Today I have seen people going to parties here. When these go to horse races, it is as if they are going to work. They have hope that maybe they will win a few cents. They have also learnt how to bet horses, and they know them well; they even know that such-and-such a horse was born of such-and-such, its grandfather is so-and-so, etcetera. Truly, some know the genealogy of horses more than their families'. But that is where they miss the point, because that does not help them to smell that today Mr so-and-so's foal will surely gallop, and show that it is a thoroughbred foal. Poor people, that is, you and I, dear friend, throw a few of our rand there, and lose, while Mr so-and-so keeps on getting richer. Is it not written that: 'Everyone who has something will be given, but he who has nothing will be deprived of what he has'?

Can't they give up, dear friend? No, they are addicted. It is like cigarette. When you have not learnt it, you wonder what pleasure these people find in it. But the day you smoke, you understand. You will never ask again. It is the same here. There is something that stimulates them, which makes a man pull out his last rand and take it there, to be consumed, but knowing well that there is no meat at home, knowing that the children are naked, that there is no . . . we are talking about something far away, he sees that his shoes have no soles, they are finished, their noses are looking at him in the eye as if they will suddenly ask him what he is actually doing! There is something that intoxicates them there; it is death, it is infectious, and never ever put your foot there. Yes, there is something that intoxicates them, which urges them . . .

Do not laugh, for that is the way of life, dear friend. There are many things that we do because we are still intoxicated by them, those that we notice the day we sober up that they were not sincere deeds but absolutely useless things. I say that life is just the same. It intoxicates us and we think that it is important; the day we sober up, the day we realize that we were chasing after a shadow, it is the day we realize the foolishness of living, it is the day we contemplate terminating it if we are not very old.

Maybe they continue because they are motivated by hope, thinking that one day they will win. Hope; ah, a great word in our lives! What can we do without hope? The one who once said this was right: 'Hope springs eternal in the human breast'[4] Because of hope they go on. They are here on Wednesday, there on Saturday; they inquire from the boys who look after the horses, they follow dreams, they slaughter beasts and say that they supplicate their ancestors, they look for voodooists . . . money keeps on vanishing. They end up no longer working, as if they have lost it up here; no longer writing home . . . sadness.

*

---

4 Alexander Pope, *An Essay on Man* (1733).

I have gone there several times. Wherever I went, I was searching, I thought I would find the joy and excitement of the derby of my childhood: song praises, ululation, real horse racing which is loved by all the Basotho, as it is in our blood as our forefathers used to race, with their cattle. But I found only robbery; I found theft that was permissible; I found joy and sadness, excitement and sorrow. The great joy that is not mixed with sadness, the joy of my childhood, that is no longer here—I cannot find it. It is now many a time that I have asked myself whether the world is getting corrupt. Most times I nearly despair. But now I have found solace that with every person, things do change. The Poet said:

'It is not now as it hath been of yore;—

Turn wheresoe'er I may,

By night or by day,

The things which I have seen I now can no more.'[5]

---

5 William Wordsworth, *Ode: Intimations of Immortality from Recollections of Early Childhood* (1807).

FAREWELL[1]

Promising someone that you will meet her at the train station is a very good thing, especially when the one that you are promising is sitting in your heart, that is, your beloved. How more pleasant it is to know that without you she will not even be able to leave the station of that big city, knowing that she will get lost? It is equally painful when you arrive there to find that your guest has not arrived; it is even worse when you know that without you, she might get lost. It is painful because you are nailed to the spot, you can't leave. But it is not that painful because you are in love, you keep hoping, you think that when she arrives she will say: 'I waited so long!' then you are thanked, or you are simply given a cursory glance, depending on your beloved's temperament. Maybe the sun will set while you are stuck there. But even if it sets it does not matter, because you will have witnessed events at the station, as I have seen myself here in Johannesburg.

*

---

1 *Tselatshweu* is an idiomatic expression, literally translating to 'have a clear or white way', i.e. travel safely.

'Greetings,[2] Mmamaswabi!'

'Look at that, Ntata Maswabi,[3] hey people! Look how thin you are? What's the matter, are you not sick? You have been away so long!'

'Am I really that thin, *mme*, it might be because of missing you?'

'Now you don't even greet the child when she greets you?' He only realized then that the child carried on the back was saying, '*Tate, tate!*'[4]

'Hello, my child. You have really grown up, hey! But why are you so dark? Is it because of basking in the sun too much?'

'You know how cold it is out there in Lesotho. It is in full swing and when the sun is warm, we bask in it . . . '

'Ah, "Lesotho, land of our fathers." '[5] That's where these travellers come from. The locomotive train travelled[6] the whole night with them, bound for the Rand. They passed towns that you know . . . Meqheleng, Bethlehem, Maokeng. You start thinking about the towns that they passed, the mountains that they saw out there at a distance, being white on their summits.

'When did you get on board?'

'Yesterday around dinner time.'

---

2 In Sesotho, the same word is by way of a greeting at all parts of the day, unlike the English variations of 'good morning', 'good evening', etc.

3 In Sesotho, a woman is referred to by her first-born, and a man by the second-born. Therefore the titles *Mme wa* [*mma*] or *ntate wa* [*ntata*]—'father of . . . ', 'mother of . . . ' or 'father of . . . ' —are used respectively, followed by the child's name.

4 *Ntate* means father, but the child articulates it as *tate*.

5 A quotation from the opening line of the national anthem of Lesotho.

6 The word *tjhutjhutsa* is an onomatopoeic rendition of the sound of a moving train.

Yesterday at that time it was fare well all over. Today they have arrived. One feels like coming closer, to ask if they did not see such-and-such a young woman getting on board, or where she disembarked. Just when you are about to ask, you remember that you may be asked if that young woman is your sibling or relative. You feel shy and you turn around. You will see when the next train arrives later in the day.

You look for a seat and you sit down. You are busy thinking about what has brought you here. You don't even see this chaos in which you are. Locomotive trains keep arriving and throwing up[7] people who come from the archipelago of towns that form Johannesburg.[8] They are alert as they disembark, like lunatics. Some jump off before it even comes to a complete halt, others jump onto it as it gathers speed. All these you don't see. You are still in a reverie.

'Jo wee! Jo wee!'[9] You jump up as you hear women screaming like that, some of them even covering their eyes. All the people are running in that direction. You also follow suit. You find a person surrounded by people. His clothes seem to have been savaged by a dog and he is covered in dust as if he was rolling on the ground. A railway police officer is holding him by the hand.

'Hey people! this person nearly caused the train to kill him, man!'

'He says what caused him to throw himself at it?' someone asked.

'His ancestors really saved him.'

'He says what caused him to throw himself at it?' another person asked.

---

7 The word used is actually 'vomiting'.

8 Upto 1994, Gauteng/Kgauteng used to refer to the City of Johannesburg. Thereafter, the name was given to one of the nine provinces where Johannesburg is located.

9 An expression of unpleasant surprise or pain.

'He says that a certain boy snatched his new hat as the train was about to move. That boy was not on board.'

'Truly some people can really kill themselves. Can a person throw himself at a train just because of a mere hat?'

'But these boys are a real nuisance. How spiteful that we are prohibited from carrying sticks! If I were to see such a thing with my stick in hand, I would crush this small head . . . and smash it!'

You go back to your seat. The old woman who is sitting next to you, who you never noticed all this time (how could you have seen her while you were busy thinking about your own trivialities?), that old woman now asks you, and now you tell her. She exclaims, and simply says: 'Hey people!, now we are in this hell of a place!' Some, who were sitting near her, who did not have anyone to meet them, are now scared—they feel really lost. They wish that they were still where they boarded the train the day before, where they were smiling when people said: 'Fare thee well!'

The sun is ascending. Time is moving. People are milling about. Some arrive carrying luggage, breathing heavily. They see a policeman and they rush to him. They ask if the train to Natal has not pulled in yet. They are told that it is about to depart and they must go up and descend on the other side. They go up running, a man telling his wife that if she dares misses it, she will know him. He has been telling her many times that they should leave home but she dillydallied! He is aware that she no longer wants to go home, because she is afraid that he will tell her father about her intractable behaviour. No sooner did they board, it pulled away, and the husband said: 'You should really thank God!'

The centipede of the road was gone, carrying those going to Natal. Tomorrow they will be in the warmth of Natal, having totally forgotten the cold weather of this place. Maybe they will be riding in another train, going up the coast or down, looking through the windows, watching the waters of the sea playing, making blue and white colours; seeing ferries, seeing forests and meadows. Tomorrow they will be seeing their sugarcane fields for making sugar; they will be seeing their round huts of Zululand; they will be seeing men walking in their loin skins only, walking with spears and shields in their hands; they will be seeing their maidens, who walk about as if they are naked, maidens who make old men get angry when someone says they are old, who make them believe that the only one who ages is one who likes to age.[10] So that they can . . .

'Fare thee well, even you who are going to Natal! Go well,[11] Shaka's children!'

An hour has hardly passed and the policeman shouts again: 'Those who are going to the Cape,[12] Port Elizabeth, going to Bloemfontein,[13] going to Lesotho, going to the Free State . . . !' as he was shouting like that, it is pulling in. It comes to a standstill, and they throw themselves inside. Oh dear, the thoughts of some of them are no longer around here, they are ahead of them. As soon as a person gets into the train, he goes to the corner and keeps silent! In this compartment, in the corner, one old man is crunched up; he is smoking a long pipe, which signifies that he is a real squire.[14] Its smell agitates other people. Even to him it is bitter in the mouth;

---

10 The author translated a Zulu idiom: *Kuguga othandayo.*

11 The author used the Zulu equivalent—*ndlelanhle*—for the Sesotho *tselatshweu.*

12 The author uses *kolone,* which translates as 'colony', which is how the eastern and West Cape were historically known—as the British Colony. The northern parts of the country were known as the Boer Colonies.

13 The author writes Mangaung, the Sesotho name formally adopted after 1994.

14 The author used a polluted version of the Xhosa word *mhlekazi* [*mohlekatsi*], which means 'sir' or 'esquire'. The Xhosa pipe, *inqawe,* is smoked by older men and women.

that is why he keeps on spitting. His thoughts are ahead of him. Maybe he is already thinking about tomorrow when he will be wearing a blanket smeared with red ochre, not actually wearing it but dragging it on the ground; maybe smoking, and his wife smoking her pipe, down in Xhosa land. He is not travelling alone. There are some of his countrymen coming on a train that is following later in the day, towards evening. He will meet with them ahead.

He is travelling with the Basotho, even though he does not understand what they are saying, because even up to this day he does not know their language. Anyone who wants to talk to him must speak his language, or keep quiet. Keep forever quiet! What do these good-for-nothing Basotho want in this train, for they heard that it is going to the Cape? Their countrymen will travel in the evening and they will meet in Maokeng or Bloemfontein. Tomorrow they will get together, they will be dancing[15] together in the red train, without bothering that they might break them. They will cross rivers together in Lesotho, climb steep hills together, leave their belongings at the same store, then proceed home and climb mountains. Their wives will come and fetch those belongings later together.

'*Tselatshweu*, children of Moshoeshoe,[16] and you grandchildren of Ntsikana!'[17]

The sun is setting. The trains[18] have gone, but they are not all gone. There is no darkness here. It is day at night because of electricity. The centipedes continue arriving and they are being announced.

---

15 The author uses the verb *hobela*. It refers to a traditional Sesotho dance called *mohobelo* which is performed by men. See Robin E. Wells, *An Introduction to the Music of the Basotho: Morija Museum and Archives* (Lesotho: Morija Museum and Archives, 1994).

16 King Moshoeshoe I (1786–1870), who reigned over Lesotho during the nineteenth century.

17 Ntsikana (1760–1821) was a Christian Xhosa prophet.

18 The author uses the word 'centipede', a Sotho metaphor for 'train'.

They are carrying away the Pedi people, the Shangaan people, where things are bad, the deserts of Botswana, Rhodesia,[19] far away, even up to the land of the Portuguese.[20] The night falls, they announce the train that is going to Lesotho, also, Lesotho and Bethlehem and Reitz and Namahadi. They announce the train that is going to Swaziland, carrying the children of Dlamini,[21] and after its departure the noise subsides. You feel physically exhausted, but you are spiritually refreshed because you have travelled to faraway countries, even though you were only here at the train station. This is what your beloved has done for you. Eventually, when you are beginning to think of going home, the policeman sees you. He beginning to realize that he has been seeing you here over a long time today. He thinks you are lost, and he asks you: 'You, *ntate*,[22] which one do you want?'

'You, *ntate*, which one are you looking for?'

'One going to the township.' He sees you smiling, and he also laughs.

'Fare thee well, son of Mokgatjhane,'[23] that is the policeman. 'Fare thee well, my countryman!' that's you.

---

19 Zimbabwe was Rhodesia before independence in 1981.

20 Mozambique was a Portuguese colony until independence in 1975.

21 Dlamini is the royal house of Swaziland, newly named Eswatini.

22 The word literally means 'father', but in this context is a polite address to an older male person, irrespective of his age.

23 Father of Moshoeshoe I.

CHANGE

Among things that torment a person there is one called longing. Have you ever heard a person saying, 'I miss home'?

At times he would resign from work, missing home without the patience of waiting for the two short weeks of holidays that he is given per year. He would be gone, because of missing home. It is right that this should be so with anyone who was well bred, who still has a place in his heart, a place where only one place reigns: his home. Blessed are those who love places where they grew up with true love, because that is the testimony that they spent their childhood well as part of their lives with happiness and joy. Which stage can surpass childhood in terms of pleasure? Cursed are those who hate places where they were born, places where they were bred, because that means that they hate their childhood.

Now you have resigned, my countryman. You have already bought a train ticket and have packed your bags. Your face is bright, for you know that tomorrow or in the future you will be far away, your home where you since left, when? A long time ago. Maybe it was the first time that you left home and it is the first time that you are returning today.

You are smiling when you think that tomorrow you will be seeing the fertile valleys of your home, you will be in your village, you will be among people in front of whose eyes you grew up, you will be among the young men and young women among whom you grew up. The whole night in the train you spend thinking about these things, sleep does not come properly.

Eventually the train hoots, you gather your baggage because the station that it is entering is your home. How long have you been seeing it in your heart? Now the time has come and your heart is beating fast. There enters the train. There is the name of the station.

You arrive home. It is written properly but there is something that does not sit well with you. It has changed, it is not the same as the day you last read it, and it is not as you used to see it in your heart. The train stops and you disembark. Now you find that you are in a strange place. You are no longer in that place that you used to see in your heart. What is the matter? It is very quiet now; you hear pigeons in the trees and other birds! No, you say perhaps it is because you are used to very noisy stations.

You arrive home. You meet children who are going to town. You don't know them, but there they are, coming to greet you. They know you. Yes, now you also remember their names; but they have grown old! You enter the village and you find it dead quiet! Houses seem to have changed. There are new ones, but even the old ones no longer look like before. You arrive home, you wonder because even the houses seem to have changed, or is it because when you left they were plastered with grey earth and there were certain patterns. Even the doors seem to have changed.

You enter the homestead and find your mother and father. It is they, there is no doubt about it; but they have changed. Grey hair has sprouted, and here and there small wrinkles show that the skin has aged over the years that have gone by. The old lady has extracted a few teeth. In the village, you find that your friends are scattered. Some are now men and women who have children, some have settled in jail; others lie in the cold, underground. Wherever you go, you miss what you were expecting, even the pool where you used to swim, it is now filled and is a little puddle where children play.

You begin to realize that what you have been missing is not this that is in front of your eyes; it is what existed, but it has now passed even though it is still present in your heart. You feel a little disappointed, because it is not pleasant to realize that what you loved has disappeared and will never come back. The time to go back arrives and you tell others at work, and say: 'Yes, it is still good, but things have changed!'

*

I was sitting in the train coming here, to Johannesburg. I was not alone; there was a woman who was also coming to Johannesburg. When the train arrived in the Vaal, another woman boarded. When she entered, I saw the other one looking at her. They eyed each other for a short while and I heard her saying: 'Are you not Mmalehlwa?'

'Greetings, *ausi*[1] Mmamookgo! Is it you that I am seeing today? Where do you come from?'

'I am from home, I since left last month. And where do *you* come from? What have you come to do here in Vereeniging? Phehello will thrash you when you arrive home late at night!' Mmalehlwa kept quiet for a moment, and giggled a little, but did not answer that question.

Mmamookgo asked again: 'How are the children, sister? I dont think I would not recognize them if I were to see them?' Mmalehlwa

---

1 *Ausi* is a Sesotho word borrowed from Afrikaans [*ou suster*], which means 'older sister'. In Sesotho, it is used as a a term of endearment or respect for a female person of any age.

kept quiet for a moment and looked at me, a bit down-hearted. I saw that she wanted to see whether I was listening. With my inquisitiveness, I pretended to be looking outside, and when I reined my eyes, I fixed them on the newspaper before me. I wanted her to narrate, without noticing that I was eavesdropping. She did exactly that.

'*Ausi* Mmamookgo, I don't know where the children are and where Phehello is. I parted ways with Phehello!'

'Don't pull my leg, *Mmannyeo!*'[2]

'Truly, *ausi*, I'm not joking.'

'Whose fault was it?' I saw tears flowing down Mmalehlwa's cheeks.

She continued and said: 'Had you asked me that question last year, *ausi*, I would have replied without hesitating that it was Phehello's fault. I saw that Phehello had changed, he was no longer the same Phehello of the days that you knew us. But you know that as months go by the truth comes out. You can deceive yourself or deceive other people today or tomorrow, but you can't deceive them or deceive yourself all these years. Today I know that it was I who was at fault . . . '

I did not listen to anything further that she said after that, as I was thinking of the words that she had just uttered. I only noticed that she was still there when she said bid Mmamookgo farewell, in Germiston. After she departed Mmamookgo said to me:

'Things do really change if it is Mmalehlwa who has parted ways with Phehello. They really loved each other!'

---

2 *Mmannyeo* literally means 'mother of so-and-so', but is also used to refer to a woman who has a child or children, and therefore bears undertones of both respect and camaraderie.

'Yes, that's how it really is. Things do change. At times they are pleasant, at times distasteful. There was an old man, I don't know whether he is dead or alive wherever he disappeared to, who used to say: "Pleasure that turns against those that it belongs to! Pleasure is mist and vapour.[3] Pain precedes joy."'

'He was right, my friend. Things change indeed.'

*

That is how it is, my compatriot. Everywhere things change, there is nothing that stands still, on the same spot. That is how they are created and there is no other way. It was said that we will be born, grow up, grow old and descend into the grave. We will have children and they will also follow that path. It is the way of change.

It right that it is so. There is nothing perfect here on earth.

Every day we try to do perfect things, we try to go where things are perfect. We are busy all the time, and every day change continues to happen. Change will come to an end the day we reach a place where things are perfect. And there is no such place except at the Creator of all, it is He who today is the same as yesterday and day before yesterday, who will be the same tomorrow and in the future.

---

3 A literal translation of a Sotho proverb: *Monono ke mohodi ke mouwane*— 'pleasure is mist, it is vapour'.

TIME

Time moves, it does not stand still. As it moves on, things change likewise, they are not standing still. In the olden days, people used to do their work without haste, only hurrying to complete it. When they hurried, it was only because they did it so that when the rain started, they would have finished ploughing, so that maize or sorghum should grow quickly and fast, so that they should not be caught by frost. Over and above that there was no hurry. If you did not succeed to start your journey today because it was raining in the morning, it did not matter because you would still leave the next day or in the future.

But today? Today things have changed. Today everything that we do we do in haste, in a hurry. We work in a hurry even though we do not know where we are hurrying to. We kill ourselves with this haste; we complain every day that we could not do this and that today, behaving as if the next day will no longer be there. By hurrying this way, we shorten our lives, we die young because we try to do a year's work in a month. For this reason, we no longer live long like our elders. But we do not notice, we think that life has just become short. This makes us hurry to complete our work before we reach the end of our lives. We see time as very brief in this world, and all of us say that we have no time! 'I haven't got time!'

This statement is used often, especially in big towns, to an extent that you can see that we use it to cover up our lies or cover up where we do not want to tell the truth because we know that it will sting. A person arrives, under pressure, to ask for help. Maybe you are the only person who can help him. He knocks at your house. Your spouse opens the door and hears everything that he needs help with. She says yes, she will tell you when you wake up. In there, you discuss this and agree with each other. When you wake up, you send a child with a letter. 'Oh, my friend, my wife told me that you would like me to come to your place, but I am very sorry that today I have got no time. . . .'

Maybe you meet your childhood friend. He made the effort because he heard that you live somewhere. He arrives at your place happy. Maybe you are also a little bit happy. Your spouse enters. You introduce her to that childhood friend of yours. She just gives him a contemptuous glance. She does not care a hoot about him, same as those that grew up with you and those who brought you up. Your friend is now leaving. Then he says: 'Don't hide yourself this way, man. You must pay us a visit. Here is my address.'

You take it but then you think of your wife. You say: 'Oh, my brother, I'll try, but there is no time here.' Sometime clock time has to tick without a clear sense, unheeded. What is it that makes us run like this, which makes us crazy?

If you take your watch out of your pocket, put it on the table as it is ticking; or when you are looking at it on your wrist, the arm going round and round, do you ever think what you are doing? Do you ever notice that the small arm keeps saying that your hour of descending into the cold earth is approaching? Do you ever notice that every hour that passes will never come back? Such thoughts make one crazy; they are scary. They are thoughts that we must never have if we want to live like sane people. But how can we elude such thoughts when we are besieged by things called watches?

Sometimes time has to pass without us seeing it clearly, without taking heed of it. We wish that it would be as if it were only yesterday where we were playing in the sand, when we got to school with grey legs, cracked feet, when we were punished! We wish as if it were only like yesterday, only to be reminded by seeing grey hair on the heads of our elders, or the children that we already have, that no, years have gone by. But even if these show us that years are gone, we are not scared because we would have spent that time, and have lived, well, without pushing ourselves by saying that we do not have time.

It is prudent to divide time into big chunks: autumn and winter, spring and summer; or when we say that the moon is waxing, or it is waning. It is pleasant when we talk about yesterday, today and tomorrow. But we cause ourselves problems when we divide the day and then start dividing the hour. A child who learns at school that sixty minutes make an hour, and that twenty-four hours make a day, does not know the dangerous thing that he is learning!

But time is dangerous only when it is divided and subdivided thus. When we think of it the way that we should, we find that it is a great thing which indeed causes great miracles. Say you are in serious trouble, your beloved father, mother, your spouse, has passed on. You find that you have come to the end of life, what is only left is for you to commit suicide because you do not see what you should live for. Maybe you loved a person very much, not conceiving that you could live without him or her. Now you receive a letter that says that he or she is no longer yours, he or she belongs to such-and-such a person. You become sad, you become confused, everything becomes distasteful to you; you do not see that truth and fidelity do exist in this world.

Years go by, when they pass by you forget those who have passed on, you even forget those who were untrustworthy. Those wounds heal and you begin to realize that those were not such serious matters. Your doctor, time, has cured you.

That is how time is. It has a way of turning enemies into friends, it can bring peace where only war reigns. Many disasters recede as time passes; yes, they recede, in such a manner that we even wonder why we bothered about them at all. Time fixes many things. We are the ones who hurry by saying that we have no time, by dividing it into several units that are useless, that only worry us.

We are worried because we want to live for a long time, as if what matters most is living for years and years, but what actually matters is to live our lives fully. To the one who lives life fully a day is just like years and years are like a day

FRIENDS

It is difficult when you have no friends. What I can say is that at all times we have friends even though sometimes it seems they are not there.

My friend, when you are born into this world, you are born with friends who are expecting you, who rejoice when you arrive, who ululate, who splash water on your father or thrash him to announce your arrival.[1]

You grow up a bit, you crawl, you walk . . . you do not crawl alone; you crawl with the boy or girl who lives in the house opposite, or your cousin. Your eyes open up to the world and you find that they are your friends.

You all grow up. You steal eggs, you break windows; you steal peaches . . . you get caught, you get thrashed. Time keeps marching on. One day you are sent to school. You go there with shiny foreheads, with clean legs, feet which have been scrubbed clean with scrubbing stones, shirts neatly buttoned up; yes, even slates that are cleanly washed, on which you are going to draw. You meet other

---

1 This is a Sotho custom: when a child is born, women splash water on the child's father to signify that it is a female; or they give him a few lashes with a stick to signify the newborn is male.

children . . . you get used to them, you change and become friends.
You grow up. Years go by. You pass your grades. Some disappear,
migrating to other villages. You continue to learn. You do not realize
that you are no longer infants; that you are growing up. You pass
Standard Six and now you have to leave your small school, this small
school that you have known for such a long time, this small school
where you have known the happiness and joy of education, yes, and
its problems; this small school that introduced you to these men of
God who taught you many things, those that today you are leaving
behind. Today, you are parting ways. My friend, today you begin to
feel fully the pain of this word: parting ways. Some are going to
other schools, while others, children of the poor, part ways with the
school that they love, to go to and work in. When the time arrives,
tears flow from your eyes. But that pain is blunted by the friendship
that existed. It seems as if it is asking if there can be a parting of
ways among those who have been friends, among those who have
pleasant years that they have spent together.

There is a great party. There are many young men and young
women. They are neatly dressed because they come from senior
schools, whose parents have sacrificed everything such that their
young siblings go naked in their families. Next to one wall stands a
certain young man who is not joyful like others. He is leaning
against the wall and he does not participate in the dancing! On his
face it is clear that his mind is not here. Some are dancing. When
two others pass by, a young woman suddenly stops next to him,
nearly tripping the young man who was dancing with her. She has
seen the young man who was leaning against the wall. He gets a
fright when he sees the young woman. The young woman pulls him
by the hand. Outside, they look at each other for a moment in
silence.

The young woman said: 'Tlala my friend, where have you been
all this time?'

'I was at home.'

'Didn't you receive my letters; I have written you so many letters?'

'I received them.'

'Tlala, why did you not reply then?'

'Paseka, I was in sorrow. My father passed on and I realized that I would not be able to go back to school because I had no one who would help me. I realized that I was out of the group of school children. I was no longer one of you now . . .'

'Tlala, I did not believe that that is what you thought about me. Was I your friend only when you were at school, only when things were okay for you? I did not know that you regard me in such low terms. Such friendship I do not really care about . . . '

'Please forgive me!'

A few second passed while they were looking into each other's eyes, their eyes shining with flowing tears.

That is how real friends are. That is how real friendship is. When things are bad, messy, as if the world has come to a standstill, not moving ahead, when everything is sour; when you feel lost, feeling as if you can carry your arms on your head and cry aloud and say, 'Oh poor me, poor child! I am in trouble!' Under such circumstances it disappears. Perhaps it is your fault, my friend, perhaps you came to this valley by mistake, in this valley, the valley of those who have been thrown outside, the valley that is teeming with crooks and the wretched, those that the world cannot choose because it does not care to do that. You feel tired, you are annoyed, you have reached a stage where you do not see why life is worth living; you feel like throwing in the towel, and parting ways with this bitter life. Just at that point, my brother, your real friends, who know you, who know all your weaknesses and what is good in you, encourage you and stretch out their hands and support you, and help you cross this terrible valley. And when you realize that there are those who think that you are still needed in this world, you get motivated, your hope grows and you are redeemed. Why should you bother about people who do not know you well, when your friends who know you still see that you are a person?

This world is cruel, my friend. Maybe in your trials and tribulations, your friends, or those that you fooled yourself into believing that they were your friends, forsake you. You feel despondent because you understand when those who do not know you desert you, but when those who know you forsake you, who will trust you? You get tired and tears do not cease on your face. But right then a miracle appears: A person appears from nowhere, I mean a person that you do not know, and does you a small favour, and awakens the little hope which was fading in your heart. That little favour rescues you. That is your friend too!

My friend, we cannot live without friends. We are weak in this world and we need those that we can lean on, those that we can support ourselves with, like walking sticks. I say, my friend, even if there is no one who sacrifices his hand so that you should lean on it, when you feel burdened by the load of life as if you will fall, when you are left alone, in that solitude, when you are quiet and meditating, you will find strength, you will feel your weaknesses dissipating because you will find another Friend. It is He Who will give you that strength because He would not have forgotten you. How can He forget you while He is watching you every day? He is your childhood friend, the one you were taught about at Sunday school, the children's Friend, the friend of all those who have fallen, no matter how; it is He who carries everyone's sins and trespasses. He still loves you even if you have forgotten Him. His friendship does not end and it does not change. He is still calling you, saying:

Come home! come home!
You who are weary, come home!
You have been wandering
Far, painfully . . .
Come home, come home
Wipe away your shame, take off sin,
Escape from bondage . . .[2]

2 A paraphrase of the hymn, 'Softly and Tenderly Jesus is Calling'.

PAPER

Even when you kick it in the street; or throw it on a trash heap or burn it, use it to ignite fire, or wrap meat in it; when you wipe your oily or greasy hands with it; I say even when you hang it in your toilet or do anything with it, oh, my friend, keep respecting it, fear it, hold it with trembling hands. Indeed, if you could afford it you must slaughter an animal for ancestors, even if it were only a little chick. Because it is very powerful even if it is weak, gets wet quickly, burns like a veld in winter and is easily foldable like a piece of cloth.

*

Western mansions have hard cement foundations, and inside, when they are really huge, they have pillars. Even makeshift houses have a tree trunk that is hoisted in the middle so that it can serve as a pillar. And it is not only houses that need to have a pillar or foundation. Many things are like that; I mean, even this tradition of the Whites that is called Western Civilization by those who practise it. It also has its foundation, which is this very same paper. Do away with paper and you will see that civilization crumbling down like ruins. Its real practitioners (not these humbugs and empty vessels who make a lot of noise every day but are just like me without understanding that civilization), when its genuine practitioners explain it, you will hear them saying that it represents certain ways about the human spirit and his humanity. But when you look closely you will see that these ways and thoughts were not born only today, some of them are ancient. Moreover, they did not come from one person's head. No, they are the fruit of fields that were cultivated by many men and women, at different epochs. One would cultivate his or her little part, and when death comes, he or she would have written down everything that he or she has learnt. The one who comes after him or her reads those, and does not start afresh but continues ploughing where the other one left off. He or she will leave it there. That is, everyone helps his or her successor a little by writing down all that he or she knows. That way the field grows.

Look carefully here then. In order to help each other, these people need to write down their works, that is, on paper.

It is not only civilization that starts here on paper. At some point in time I once went to a hillock where a person could see parts of Johannesburg well when he was on it. And when I was there, I saw trains that were running on rails, trams that were flowing smoothly, cars driving on the road and thundering motorbikes; I was watching aeroplanes that were flying over many beautiful tall buildings. As I was watching all these, a thought struck me: that all these were born out of paper. Before all of them were made or built ,they had plans, that is, they were neatly drawn on paper until they were complete. It was only then that their makers were able to start fabricating them with steel, following drawings that were already complete on paper.

How many things are born of paper? My friend, it can start a war or sue for peace, because it can spread mutual hatred or love among peoples. Perhaps today we go to bed thinking of our problems, without hating anyone. The next day when we wake up, we find that newspapers have revealed the truth that we did not know, which is that all the problems that are facing us, even your poverty, is deliberately caused by the . . . nation, an arrogant nation that wants to destroy your nation. Do you agree that your nation should be annihilated so easily? Not at all. Hmm, you begin to realize that the . . . nation is so evil! You must prepare to fight—there is no alternative! The war is on. Even the day it ends, the situation remains the same. You are still soldiers, you are facing it, you are prepared to die for your country, which the . . . want to destroy. You wake up one day and you hear the very same newspaper saying that blood has been spilt, it is enough, and now the . . . will no longer undermine you, they have felt that you are men; even though there is no truce yet, the war must cease, and other ways of solving problems with the . . . must be found. The newspaper has spoken, and after a week the war is over.

I have heard it many times, a person saying that he finds it easier to write to another person what he wants to say instead of talking to him, face to face. Now I still believe that this is the situation with some people. When they have quills in their hands, they are eloquent, but when they do not have them, they are deaf mutes. But if they knew that what you have written down is evidence that will never be forgotten or denied even when you who have written it no longer agree with what you once wrote. That is why nowadays when something is discussed with someone, perhaps after mutual agreement, you see him shoving a pen to you and saying that you must sign your agreement. They know the power of paper. In most cases, we live with a person knowing him as a person of this nature; that we really respect. One day he passes on. We praise him at his funeral. Books are written about him, books that eulogize him. A year passes, or two, three or even ten years. After that period of time, a historical researcher discovers this person's letters somewhere. In these letters we discover the weaknesses of that stalwart, which we did not know, which were perhaps known only by his bosom friend. We begin to be surprised, but then it is too late. That is the way of paper. It is your eternal voice that continues to speak even when you are in the cold earth, when the tongue has turned into worms. Through it you speak even when you are dead!

*

I once met an old man with his hands on his head, weeping, tears flowing down his face and he was saying: 'Puseletso, my child! Are these your actions?' I was going to see a certain man who was an attorney. When I arrived, I found him with his back towards the door, holding a handkerchief, also wiping tears from his eyes. When he heard me entering, he turned around and waved at a chair with his hand, and only said: 'It is because of these children of ours! Today it has happened to this poor old man, tomorrow it will be me and you!'

'What has his child done?'

'He has passed on . . . '

'But that is the way for all of us . . . '

'If he had just died, we would not be very troubled. The problem is what he has left behind.'

'What has he left behind?'

'He left a piece of paper. On that piece of paper, he has written that all his belongings he bequeaths to his wife. Today that so-called wife is up in arms, and is chasing the poor old man away. She says it is her house. Had it been a house that she had worked for with that husband of hers, it would be no big deal. But the house was built by that poor old man, on a site that he bought for himself through the sweat of his brow. He trusted his son and trans-ferred it to his name . . . he did not think, I also did not think, that such things would happen. But there we are! There is a piece of paper . . . '

There is a piece of paper! 'Puseletso, my child! Are these your actions?' There is a piece of paper, Puseletso is still talking, Puseletso is still present. 'Puseletso, my child!' I also found myself with tears flowing down my cheeks.

EXAMS

I will never forget the first test that I wrote in my life. When I say that I wrote it, I am not telling the truth because we actually did not write it. I remember that day very well, because it is the first day at school that I remember. I am told that I went to school with my sister, and played with her. I think I must have learnt at that very time, while playing with—a, e, i, o, u. I see that is the day when things became clear in my eyes. I remember very well when my name was called and we were made to stand outside. We were told to read. I remember, that day I saw letters as words and read them easily. Even up to this day, when I think of that day, I really feel that a miracle happened. What is it that was in my head that made letters become visible as words, which is what other children could not do? Could it be that there was something in my head, which helped me, which 'copied for me'?

After we read about the antelope, guinea fowls and partridges, we were told to stand in a queue, and I was at the tail end because of my 'height'. From there we were led to the classroom where the principal taught. I was glad to see my sister there. I thought that they had brought me to her. In the evening, I was totally surprised when the principal told my mother that I would also need a reading book. Cobwebs were now off my eyes. I had passed the first test.

It is a long time ago, my friend. As years went by, I contended with other tests. But now I again found something new . . . fear. It is the fear that you may perhaps fail in your work, especially when you feel that you are weak at your work—and who would be so vain such that he feels that he knows his work? Even if he knows it, he starts by asking himself questions . . . will he pass the way that he wishes?

When fear gets into us, my friend, it is only then that we feel our weakness deeply; it is only then that we notice that we have no strength and we need help. Many times have I heard a person shouting in bed, with a voice louder than the psalm: 'I will lift up mine eyes unto the hills, from whence cometh my help. My help cometh from the Lord, who made heaven and earth!'[1]

I said in my heart: 'That is a Christian child!' Most of the time, some repeated the English poet's words: 'More things are wrought by prayer than this world dreams of!'[2]

Prayer, my friend, is a great thing. I also prayed, praying in the examination room before I raised my quill to answer questions. Perhaps I was making a mistake by praying only when I was in trouble. All of us are like that. Which child would ask his father to help him do what he can do by himself? But up to this day I am grateful because I learnt to pray when I am doing a difficult task—there are so many difficult tasks in a person's life! Is life itself not work?

Hear me, my friend. When I say that I was praying in the examination room, I do not mean that I wanted to be helped with things that I had not studied. No, those that I did not know were through my fault, because I did not use the gift that I was given by the Creator, which is my brain, and also the opportunity of being at school. No, I was asking for strength to defeat the fear that was in

---

1 Psalm 121:1–2.
2 Alfred Lord Tennyson, *Mort d'Arthur* (1912).

me, strength to be able to use everything that I had learnt. I was asking God to give me strength to close the gap of weakness that appeared in my soul. And indeed, when I finished, I felt peace coming back to my heart, I stopped trembling and started thinking the way I usually did. And that is an important thing in the exam. Many people have failed because of fear, trembling, not thinking as they usually do on a daily basis, forgetting things that they know, such as their names, things that they remember when they leave the exam room.

Because things that happen in the exam room are very strange, my friend. You enter and start fighting, because it is a real battle. When questions are facing you perhaps you smile, because you know only that which is required of you. Maybe you are blank, totally blank; sweat breaks on your brow, even in the middle of winter when it is cold. You perhaps feel like going to the loo, even though you might have gone there before going into the exam room—you look around, this way and that way. Eventually you surrender. Perhaps you know all the answers to an extent that you are unable to choose. A minute passes without you knowing what to do. You start. You race. Is that old thing up there still on time or is that old man moving it forward because he is in a hurry to go home! You pull out your own watch (because yours will always be a real watch)—but today it too is fighting against you. Hey people! time is a crook! You head is still full and you want to release every-thing that you know but—but time, time is against you! What was the purpose of studying if you are not given time to pour out a bit for these examiners, so that they could see that your cup is full and overflows? You become angry. Time is still galloping. 'Five minutes more!' My God! There is a question that you have hardly touched! Even though you know it like bread! Who will you tell this? Who will believe? Even you, sweat is breaking and you feel like going to the loo! But you want to get a first-class pass. You all stop. You all leave. So-and-so is sitting there stubbornly. What is the matter? Outside you hear that the poor child messed himself up. That is the exam.

The exams are over. Schools have closed and you are all now at home. When you finished the exams, you felt that you had passed because what you wrote was still fresh in your head. But now days are going by, you forget them, and your passing and your failing seem to be the same thing, something that might happen with sheer luck! Fear comes back once again and it keeps growing, because the day on which the names of those who have passed are published in the newspapers is approaching. You start praying again, you who have been sleeping and waking, without knowing that the Lord God of hosts still exists. Today you kneel down: 'From whence cometh my help?'

With trembling hands, with loose knees, with a heart that is beating painfully, with breathing that is like a dog's after running; yes, with eyes full of tear drops, you open the newspaper which carries the names. Oh, could it be that . . . could it be . . . You start searching again because you did not see your name . . . your friend is right next to you, and he sees it. 'Oh, man, what's wrong? Is this not your name?' You blink several times, tears fall, tears of joy!

You run home like mad! You are praised everywhere. You are happy, but is there something that you have forgotten? 'I will lift up mine eyes unto the hills, my gratitude will be directed there, to Jehovah who has created them.' That is what you must utter . . . we only know how to ask, we do not know how to give, even through gratitude!

Years have gone by, my friend, very many of them. Exams have come and also passed . . . or have they indeed passed? Yes, perhaps they have passed, but there is only one that remains. The one that remains has been there since you were born, it will end the day you die; that exam will tell whether you join the sheep or go to the goats,[3] a very tough test, my friend. Maybe we are also weak in its face. Let us pray every day, and ask for strength that will support us when we are weak . . . because we are weak, my friend. We know from whence our help will come.

---

3 Biblical imagery for Heaven (sheep) and Hell (goats).

THE RIVER

My home is on the border between Lesotho and Free State. When I opened my eyes, I already knew how to say, 'Lesotho is on the other side of the Caledon River.' It is something that I knew so well, just like drinking water or eating. It was something that I was used to. And when you are used to something, my friend, it is not often that you think of it. You start thinking about it a lot only when it disappears or when you arrive where it does not exist. Isn't it that even this mysterious thing that we call life, we are so used to it that we do not think about it? But the day one of us kicks the bucket, it is only then that we ask ourselves what it is exactly that went out of him.

That is how it was with me. I never thought that there could be any other boundary between two countries except a river. I had already visited the Cape Colony. When I left Free State, I found a huge boulder of a river called Orange River, which was a boundary when one crosses into the Cape Colony. After I came back from the Cape Colony, I prepared to go Johannesburg, and there I found that Transvaal was separated from Free State by the Vaal River. In another year I went to Natal, thinking of holidaying at the sea. I thought that I would see the boundary between Natal and Transvaal, because I used to hear my fiend saying that the border is a small wooden notice written 'NATAL' on one side, and on the other 'TRANSVAAL'. I did not believe it, just as much as I did not believe what was written in the atlas. But I was unfortunate because the train passed that place at night.

A few days ago, I got a big fright. I was going to Swaziland. I was driving a car, my small map told me that we were approaching, and I stopped, got my documents ready and proceeded. In my head I was already imagining a river, and a bridge, and on the other side of the bridge a Customs office and next to it a pole wearing a Swaziland flag. While I was imagining these things, I suddenly saw 'You are now in Swaziland.' I stopped the vehicle. I looked back, because I thought that I had missed the river. I found nothing, I mean not even a neatly woven little fence. I stood there surprised.

No, today I am no longer surprised. I also know why nations keep on fighting, quarrelling over boundaries. It is because of such borders. These things are not even boundaries; they are just a mockery. The day they want to pick up a fight, one will wake up and yank that useless pole from the ground, and hoist it ten miles from where it was, and then war starts. Yes, today I know that the real boundary of peace between countries is a river. Today I know why the French and Germans keep quarrelling about 'natural boundaries', which is the Rhine River. A river is the real boundary. Today I understand why people talk about 'the Jordan Valley . . .' as the hymn says. Jordan separates earth and heaven and I remember pictures that I used to see in many families when I was still a child (nowadays I no longer see them, as I enter this and that house I see the picture of the head of the household and his wife standing pompously!), pictures of people disappearing in the Jordan, and when they appear yonder they appear wearing clothes that are as white as snow.

*

When you are standing on the bank of a river, you see yourself reflected twice, my friend. You do not only see your shadow, but you see your humanity and that of other people, because a river is just like us. Where you are standing, you see water flowing, passing by. You do not know where it comes from, and where it is going, where it has passed, what it has done on the way; you do not know where it is flowing to and what it will do on the way; who it will help and where it will end up. Life also flows that way. I say, just like the person that you meet at the crossroads—which you do not know where he is going, where he comes from, what he does and where he will end up.

It does not resemble a person only through its flow, but even humanity exists in it. When you are standing at the bank of a river, you think it is deep, my friend, whereas it is only a puddle. Or you think that it is not deep because the water is clear and you can see rocks at the bottom . . . whereas these rocks are not close. When it is empty, it makes a lot of noise on stones, like a person who has shallow knowledge and annoys us with self-praise. When it is full, it flows without making noise, like a real expert who does not make noise about his knowledge. When you are standing there on the bank of the river, it is like travelling with a person that you do not know what is in his heart, because even with the river, you do not know whether it is teeming with fish or snakes, mythical snakes.

There is also treachery in it. Boys get there, and just play; they cross over to the other side and they come back happy. Suddenly when they are in the middle of it, they feel the water getting stronger, reaching up to the neck, whereas earlier it reached below the waist. They get frightened and lose their swimming skills. One of them drowns. You rush there, and when you get there you find the river full, flowing quietly, the water reaching above the banks, as if it is licking its lips, but without saying what is has done with the child.

When a child is born, in most cases we have hope that it will grow up, become a real man or a real woman, even though we mostly forget that that hope can only be realized if we bring him or her up like a person. The same applies with the river. It starts off as a little well, here and there. It grows, and becomes a streamlet, and the streamlet becomes a stream. I already know the Orange River up there, on the Maluti,1 and it is not the same as the rock that we see when we go to the Cape, coming from Mangaung.

Recently, when I crossed the Vaal when I was going to Swaziland, without knowing that I was crossing it, thinking that I was crossing a rivulet. But the river also brings hope; it brings life to those who can use it properly.

But like all other things in the world, it flows, it passes, it does not stand still. The person who wants to use it must do so right now, otherwise it simply passes, as a river. Time and the river are similar. Time is also a river, it is the same thing; yesterday and today are the same thing, because they are not separate, and the river also testifies . . .

When you are standing at the bank of a river, you hear it flows loudly on stones, or where it has formed a waterfall, you listen, and listen carefully, eventually it would seem like it is talking, it is speaking an ancient language, it sings a song which has been heard by generations, a song which perhaps Shaka's[2] armies, Mzilikazi's[3] and the Tlokwa[4] people heard while they were taking a break, after quenching their thirst. You feel yourself close, covering hundreds of

1 This refers, in the plural (singular: *leluti*) to the range of mountains in Lesotho, but is also a common noun for 'mountain(s)'.
2 Shaka Zulu (1787–1828) is the nineteenth-century warrior who became king, unified the scattered peoples and formed the Zulu nation.
3 Mzilikazi (1790–1868) was one of Shaka's military leaders, who defected across the river that divided present South Africa and Zimbabwe, and established his kingdom of Matebeleland.
4 A group led by a female regent, Mmanthatisi, from 1813 to 1824, who were later absorbed into the Sotho nation by King Moshoeshoe I.

past years, and those hundreds and hundreds feel like yesterday, as if
the sentinel of those armies would appear right now . . . you feel as
if time is standing still here, you feel as if thousands of years are but
a day and a day is like thousands of years. You begin to understand
what is always said by the Creator of things . . .

DRIVING AN AUTOMOBILE

When you are watching a person driving a car, you can think that it is a really easy thing. Indeed, it is so with a person who knows how. You can also affirm that even learning how to drive a car is easier than learning how to ride a horse. You drive comfortably, sitting on a soft seat, from which you will never fall, because you have shut the doors, you are sitting indoors. But the horse is different, because you sit up there without being protected by anything, without even a saddle, perhaps it is emaciated and its back is scraping you. When it starts moving, bumping and bumping, you start dancing like a sack on it, you want to hold on to something and you grab it by its mane, holding on tight for life and death; it does not help at all and you look down where you are going to fall; you start becoming dizzy before you even fall. But a car is different.

It is a different story if you have not touched that steering wheel. The day you touch it, you will tell a different tale, my friend. You will find it refusing to go straight, prancing, going this way and that way. You will find that this house in which you are sitting is intractable. You look at your instructor who is sitting next to you (he is still driving, while you are only controlling the steering wheel to learn how to direct it to go straight). I mean, you look at him, and he tells you, laughing lightly: 'It's you who is steering this wheel.

Just hold it, you will see that this Whiteman's thing is able to stretch itself and sniff the road, such that where the road turns slightly it is not necessary for you to turn it much.' You do not believe but you listen and eventually realize that it is true, the truth that you did not realize when you were sitting next to the driver watching him driving.

Today you are behind the wheel; you know how to handle the wheel carefully so that you can go straight, not imitating a drunkard. A new problem is at your feet. You saw the driver treading and releasing, the Whiteman's thing is simply flowing. But with you it seems not to be agreeable to you. You want to look at your feet so that you can see what you are doing. Your instructor: 'No, just look ahead where this thing is going. This thing has lights but it has got no eyes. Eyes are yours. You will cause it to capsize. Just step on without looking, my friend.' You start, step on the clutch, you pull the gear down, you raise the clutch the way that you were told but . . . 'Lord of peace! . . . why is thing jerking like that!' It is still jerking a lot; you hold tight onto the steering wheel—now you think that it is the reins of a horse and you think that you are pulling back the house in the mouth so that it should stop. Today you are fooling yourself, this is another type of horse! 'Step on the clutch, man,' so says your instructor. Then the car stops. You pull out your handkerchief, you wipe away cold sweat from your forehead and your legs are shaking.

*

Days pass. You get used to it and you get a licence to prove that you can drive. You start driving calmly. As time goes, you get more used to it, and your fear subsides, and attention dissipates. That is how it is, my friend, people who cause accidents are not learners but it is those who already know how to drive, those who can sleep behind the wheel while the car is moving. One day, when you are absent-minded, an accident occurs. You get a fright. You wake up from the sleep in which you were. You start realizing the truth that you did not realize when you started learning how to drive. A person who sits behind the wheel is driving beside his casket. A sad thing is that he may die out of no fault of his, my friend. He will be killed by a drunkard who is driving another car. It is we who will later see that it was not your fault, it was that drunkard's, but as for you, you will be dead, lying in the cold earth. It is painful to think of such, let us drop the subject.

Now you are driving properly. Perhaps you even got a job as a truck driver, or a bus driver, or as a wealthy man's chauffeur. You wear a black uniform; on your hands you wear pure white gloves— and you drive feeling that you are so-and-so's son or a noteworthy person. Even those who see you passing by feel like greeting you . . . I once met an old man riding a horse. When he saw the car that I was approaching in, he prepared himself to greet me and held the visor of is hat. I felt that I also had dignity. Just as I was preparing to greet him, I saw him pulling his face, and the grin on his face vanished, and he seemed to be getting angry. He was not aware that I was not white, as he had thought. People don't smile at you; they do not greet you if you are not white, if you are black. I also hear that Satan is black! But a car changes things, including your skin. I was still thinking about that man when I heard a child shouting next to the road: '*Tata mulumbi*!'—Father Whiteman! I smiled, because I really love being treated like royalty.

I mean, I was on a journey when these things happened, because it is pleasant driving on a journey, especially on good roads, at night, with a breeze of fresh air outside. Your windows are shut, your dashboard is glowing and your lights are bright ahead of you; in front, the engine is talking; it cries, it sings, it devours the fields, streams and hills. What a pleasure, my friend! But if you were to stop, you would not think that it was that engine which was singing pleasantly. In the wilderness, in the dark, you are alone! My friend, I will narrate these on another day but not today, because tomorrow I am hitting the road early. I am going to Mozambique. If I talk about such things, I will end up not leaving.

THE SEA

When a road winds itself like a snake, descending, ascending, bending around bends, appearing suddenly from forests, and it is everywhere, way ahead grey sea water is visible, like a big mound; and all in front of you looking like they are full of joy, even the car that you are driving was heating up with sound, now seems to be singing, it is no longer rumbling; it is even refusing to stop, because even when you try to rein it in it keeps going at a great speed; when the train that you are travelling in no longer makes audible sound, it is like a horse that is wide eyed, and when it whistles it expresses the joy that is in its heart—when all these are happening, you feel your heart full of peace and happiness and joy because you know that you are victorious, you have conquered the road, you have reached its end, the road that you have been asking yourself, when it disappeared around a mountain—or field or hill—where does it end. Today you know, because you have conquered it.

You do not stop in that town. No, you forge ahead; you want to reach the end of all the town roads. You are going to the beach. You stop there in surprise. You find yourself standing on sand. Here at your feet water advances and recedes as if it is playing, it is alive. It is making a loud noise and a lot of foam when the waves break on the sand. And as they break that way and rush to the sand, they brings a miscellany of things and small shells, big shells, beautiful ones and grotesque ones, little animals that you see for the first time, ones which make you shrink, even fish of all kinds; because the sea is carrying a heavy burden.

In the middle you see waves forming many little moving ditches, until they stop right here at your feet. But beautiful little ditches, deep green! Here and there, you can see white things which look like white goats on a mountain when they are pure white, their hairs washed by rain—it is foam formed by waves which collide with each other and fade there. When you look carefully, they look like goats that emerge suddenly and then vanish! Far away, you see the sea, as if it is rising and meeting the sky. How is it out there in the sea when a person is watching these living waters, right there and far away from the land? You ask yourself. Before you finish asking yourself, your thoughts are chased away by the noise that is near you. Because every day there are tourists. Some take a dive into the waves before they scatter and they feel good when they hit them upside down, pulling them into the sand, and they go home with their hair full of sand, exhausted, hungry, happy ('because strange are the things which make us happy'). Some run naked or wearing only loin skins. I mean, here even Africans who are shy of walking naked, here you find them lying on the sand, scorched by the sun! Some are running around. They are all happy because that is what has brought them here. I mean, even the money that took years to save is spilt just like that, easily as if a person picked it up like shells from the sea. Here every hour that passes is full of joy and happiness, which amounts to decades in other places.

Even when you walk around town, you feel the same ambience. It is as if the town is uttering words like: 'Eat, drink and be merry, for tomorrow you may die.' The whole town really lives to give you everything that evokes pleasure; its inhabitants live for that; they are your slaves. You see in their eyes that they are wondering at you.

Indeed, they must. They say that you are fortunate because you know where the road from your home country ends. Where it ends for you, as far as they are concerned, that is where it starts because they do not know your home country!

You watch everything in this village. Eventually you arrive where ships unload people and cargo. You find ships belonging to many nations with their flags hoisted on them. You feel closer to faraway countries. You see cargo being offloaded; another being loaded. Goods of many kinds, and live cattle. You start asking yourself where they are going. While you are still wondering, you hear a song on that end. You head that way. You find that it is an English warship, sailing away. You see Englishmen wearing their white uniforms, standing still as if they are not people, white stones, lifeless. The anthem has ended, there it is, sliding away slowly as if it is reluctant to go. While they are standing there, these children of the English, they raise their hats to salute those remaining behind. Right on its front, on the bow, someone stands there. He is not facing the world; he has his back to it now, his thoughts are already in the sea where they are heading. The poor child is looking at it wistfully, as if it is calling him. He knows it, he loves it. 'I wish I were him,' that is you saying that.

You start thinking about the vastness of endless waters, turbulent waters, and the sky up above, stars at night, days without end, and eventually the earth emerges again. And you see a hamlet, after it the road again . . . because the road has no end. You go back home feeling disappointed, defeated. (Because that is how life is, my friend. Today you are victorious, the next day you are defeated.) You go back home saying: 'One day I will make it across . . . ' That is what you believe will happen. Where would we be without hope?

THE HOSPITAL

Many people are so scared of hospitals that a person tends to stay at home until the illness is so deeply rooted that by the time he gets to hospital he will be in serious trouble, to an extent that the day he starts recovering, if he ever does recover, he would not know how he got to hospital in the first place. Many people go to hospital only to die there, to increase the number of people who die in hospital, to give hospitals a bad name. 'So-and-so and so-and-so died in hospital, hospitals kill people.' But the truth is that they killed themselves by not going to the the hospital in time. People fear the hospital. Most people wait until they are at death's door, moaning in the final throes: 'Lethola is ill, *he is in hospital!*'

Time for visiting patients is not long in most hospitals. It can be about only two hours. Most of the time when we get there, we find that everywhere it is dusted and clean, beds have been made neatly and patients are sleeping on white bedspreads; it would seem that they are preparing themselves to enter the state of being angels. Some of them sleep at this time, even though at other times they would be jumping about and making noise. Their relatives find them quiet, sleeping, not moving much, looking like people who are really sick; even when they speak, they do so with exhaustion, without strength. When I say this, I remember a certain man who would become seriously ill whenever he saw his wife coming. He would really fall ill, and moan seriously, confusing other patients and nurses who did not know his ways. But that was only a trick to confuse his wife. He thought that if he did not do that, she would pester him with trivial domestic problems and suggest that he come back home because he has recovered, even though the doctors have not said so. Now the wife will think that nurses are cruel because they are not concerned about her husband's groaning, and she will go home bearing a grudge against the hospital, because of how badly patients are treated.

When we get into hospital, we find patients lying on white bed-spreads, and we think that they are all angels. The truth is that we feel sorry for them, we feel pity for them to such an extent that we cannot conceive that they may be cheating, because they seem to be very ill! Indeed, that is how it is. When they get into hospital, they are sick and at death's door, and when they are tired, they are meek like God's children. Some of them remain in that state of meekness even when they have recovered, until they are discharged. But people are different. Some, when they feel that they are getting stronger, start complaining. A person starts to realize that the food that is served is not real food, the food that he eats at home is better (even though at home his staple food is perhaps porridge made of yellow maize). He starts realizing that the medicine that is prescribed for him is not medicine but polluted water. He starts asking the nurse what sin he has committed because when she gives others an injection he does not get one (because the doctor has not prescribed it). The one who is being injected starts realizing that the nurses jab him painfully, spitefully. Some of them go to the extent of assaulting the nurses.

That does not mean that there are no nurses who deserve to be beaten up. How can there be a dearth of such when there are so many lunatics among them? Among these are those who are provocative at all times, who think that all the patients are actually not sick but pretending; who say that patients think that they have come to a hotel and not a hospital, who run out of impatience to an extent that they slap a weak patient just because she has asked for something that she has the right to ask for; who lack respect so much that they no longer know that words like 'mother' or 'father' are used even when talking to people who are not your biological parents; who burst out and call people who are their father's age names like John.

No wonder they behave so badly. They have new mothers, who are grass-eating lunatics of inspectors. As far as these inspectors are concerned, all the patients are lazy and all the nurses are angels (or are angels until they quarrel with them). They only care for cloths, bedding, walls, nurses and their assistants, as if hospitals are built for them but not for patients. If ever a patient talks back to an arrogant nurse, these inspectors will make it a point that that patient is discharged without a disciplinary hearing or sentence passed. Florence Nightingale would be ashamed if she were to see them.

They have not only spoilt nurses, but they have also spoilt nurses' assistants—cleaners and porters. These have also turned themselves into enemies of patients, or their lords. I remember one who told a disabled patient who needed a chamber pot to take it easy, which meant that he should hold on until she knocks off and the next shift or workers clock in. When those arrive, you will hear one of them saying: 'Hey people! why didn't this one relieve himself all this time, and when I arrive it is only then that he wants to . . . !' And if the patient comes to a point where he loses control, there will be loud howling!

When I think of nurses, I am not thinking about these ones. I am thinking of children of dignified people, who were brought up decently, who have patience, who have respect; those who touch you with care and respect when they touch you, because they realize that you are in pain; who realize that your thoughts are confused; who realize that you need peace and they should alleviate your plight. My friend, there are such nurses. When they arrive in the morning, they come happy and talk to you pleasantly, smiling, trying to make you happy, to forget what is eating you, trying to give you courage, to show that this world of Jehovah was created for us and we must live in happiness, and rejoice for the life that he has given us. What more can cure a person more quickly than the knowledge that life is a great gift that we have been given by the Creator? When they arrive in the morning, they come in happy and they infect you with that happiness. They come to you and ask you how you went through the night. When they see that you are sad, they come, talk to you, you unwind and start chatting. When you are scared and think that your sickness is very bad, they tell you about the sicknesses that they have seen, and you begin to realize that yours is nothing. The day they are absent, you feel lonely.

You get used to them, and you trust them. Eventually, you find that they are like your siblings, like your mothers. When your relatives come, they find you happy. They also get excited when they see that you are getting help. They do not know the source of your peace, what they only see is that the hospital is treating you well.

Perhaps you are married and your spouse is crazy. He sees that you are just too happy, and that you are no longer ill, you are just relaxed because . . . he gets you discharged! There are many who get cruelly discharged that way by their spouses. But that does not bother the nurses; they only perform their duties! It is not surprising that many bachelors propose marriage here! These are the true daughters of Florence Nightingale, who make her smile where she is sleeping. They will make people love the hospital and go there before they become seriously ill. They are our hope.

But you know that people tend to revenge themselves not on people who have offended them.[1] It is painful to see some patients bullying such nurses, avoiding lunatics, avoiding cruel ones and going for kind ones,[2] scared of their cruelty and going for kindness.[3] That is how the world goes.

The same applies to doctors. There are many boys (some of them are men who refuse to grow up) who think that the hospital is a picnic. They walk about in white coats with stethoscopes in their pockets or hanging around their necks and feeling good when they are respected by patients and nurses, even when they are doing nothing. Some feel good when they talk about other people's diseases, using long words, without thinking much about helping a patient but only thinking about what they are going to learn about the patient's disease.

There is such a type, my friend. Treating a person because you are aware that she is ill, because you want to help her, is different from treating her without thinking of her pains, without thinking that she is a person, thinking only that you have found an opportunity to learn about a certain disease that you will write about so that your name can be famous, to be respected by other doctors. Such are recognizable when talking to patients. As far as he is concerned, they are not human; as far as he is concerned, they may as well be mice or monkeys that are infected with certain diseases, so that people can learn about those diseases from them.

---

1 The author uses a Sesotho proverb, which literally translates as 'it [a cow] does not pay revenge on one that has gored it' [but another].
2 The author uses a Sotho idiomatic expression: 'being scared of hot porridge [lehala] and going for cool porridge [moratha]'.
3 Another Sotho idiomatic expression: 'being scared of hot spinach and going for mild spinach'.

But there are also some who study those diseases, but do not do so simply because they are thinking about the fame that they will get, but are inspired by the love that is in their hearts, the love that makes them keen to reduce diseases and plight from which their people are suffering. Mostly they do not find rest until they die. That is why the names of the famous in the field of medicine belong to such people.

When a patient is admitted into hospital, you can recognize them. They try very hard to explain the patient's disease to the relatives, and promise that they will try by all means humanly possible to help him. When the relatives leave the hospital, they leave with courage, feeling that they have left their child in good hands. He talks in the very same manner to the patient so that he can have hope, knowing that they will try everything. When there is hope, my friend, the patient has already started to recover.

Just look at him when he has lost his patient. When the patient's relatives arrive and get into his office, they find him also sad, obvious that death has touched his heart. He will start by explaining to the patient's relatives how he tried, how he was gaining hope and how his hope changed to naught. He condoles with them, and they see that the time had come because all the help that was provided was in vain. They go home despondent but understanding, also knowing that if in future they would have another sick person they will bring him here, to this genuine friend . . . this grandchild of Hippocrates.

When a patient has recovered fully, you can see their joy. You will find them happy, joyful as if it is their friend who has recovered. When you leave, they pat you on the shoulder, happy for you, together with their nurses, as if they are witnessing a miracle. Perhaps in your heart you feel sad because you are parting ways with people that you seem to have known for a very long time, who are now friends. That is how it is, genuine friends that are found in moments of trouble, do not take a few years to leave you.

You part with them happy, and sad. The same applies to them but they quickly forget, because as soon as you exit through that door another one enters, who is at death's door, who needs their attention . . . As for you, you leave healthy, happy, perhaps asking yourself what exactly it is that makes people fear the hospital whereas you found friends there!

PLANTS

It is difficult to understand the saying that a person can have eyes but not see. But that is how it is. There are not many who think that plants are alive. When we think of plants that are alive, it is only when we think of plants such as maize or sorghum or spinach that we plant in our gardens. Even then, when we say that they are alive, we simply mean that they grow. That is the word we use frequently, because the life of plants is not life that is similar to one that we mean when we say a person is alive or an animal is alive. We take it for granted that it is different. Maybe that is because they do not walk, they do not cry, they have no eyes, ears, mouths, etcetera.

On the other hand, it is good that we do not take it that they are alive, like us, that they also feel pain. We regard it as a different matter altogether. Do you think that there would ever be a woman who would take a knife, get into her garden a pick sprouts or beans without trembling? Most people do not refuse to do that, much as they refuse to slaughter a chicken. Which young man would put a flower on his jacket and go to propose love? He would be rejected, being seen as cruel, that he has no heart because he has killed a flower! Picking a sprout of onion would be just like cutting a lamb's shank while it is still alive and leave it so that it can heal and grow again. We would have no place to walk or lie down lest we hear grass saying: 'Ouch! You are squashing me, you human being!' There would now be an organization that challenges those who commit transgression of plant rights.

But the truth is that they are alive, like you and I. They breathe even though they have no lungs. That does not help because even fish have no lungs but they inhale clean air and exhale polluted air. Plants do that too. Moreover, just like us, they are not sitting with their arms folded, they work and make themselves food because their food is not made for them like me and you and an animal, who eat the sweat of other people's brows. Some of us are like plants. They make their own food and we just go and harvest without contribution.[1] They begin the work of making food early in the morning when light shines, until light disappears in the evening. They, like you and me, are able to save food that they do not need today, for future days. In this regard, they surpass many animals.

But even among animals there are those that are lazy, who cannot work for themselves, that are prepared to live through cheating and robbery. They let others grow, and when those are big enough, they just grow on them; their roots anchor themselves in the stems of others and suck all the nutrients that are in turn sucked from the soil by the roots of those plants, and eventually kill them. Because even among plants fighting each other, trying to kill each other, is a big thing. When you get into a forest, and look carefully, you will find that even though it is quiet, there is a big battle going on. Some kill others just as we have said; others loop themselves around others without killing them simply wanting to reach out to the light; others climb onto others using their thorns. Some have learnt the truth that many people, yes, and many nations, have not noticed, that helping each other is more beneficial than fighting each other.

---

1 A Sotho idiomatic expression: 'eating wild fruit that has been prepared for you' [without your contribution].

One plant gives to another something it does not have, and the recipient in turn gives the benefactor what it does not have. They live in peace. What admirable wisdom!

Plants know how to lay traps. They trap ants and they ensnare them. I did not believe that until I saw a certain shrub in Natal. Some of its leaves look like a hand; they even have little sticks that resemble fingers. An insect is attracted by the colour of this 'hand', and when it perches on it is trapped by sticky liquid. As it tries to wriggle out of the fingers, the hand rises, and eventually the insect finds itself caught by strong a hand, as if being clasped. The day the insect's body has been sucked dry by that hand, it opens up and whatever is left is blown away by the wind. It is not only this plant that can trap insects. There are many others which catch in various ways, which show real genius, such that I often thank our Creator that there are no plants that lay traps that way that are as huge as trees, because they would finish our children! Truly, my friend, not only children but also adults, especially elderly ones, because plants have force of attraction.

When they call, there is no one who can resist. When they have blossomed, with colourful flowers, insects, bees and butterflies do not rest; they run the whole day, perching here and there, looking for pollen on flowers, because they are attracted by the beautiful colours of plants. By doing that, they fulfil they role of plants, that of mixing male and female so that seeds can be born. We are also attracted by the colours of flowers, such that we pick them and put them in our houses on or our jackets.

The desire of plants also gets fulfilled that way, even when there are seeds that have to be scattered, spread across the field, so that they should not grow in one place. Birds which eat wild fruit or sweet fruit, monkeys that pick fruit, the wind that scatters hairy seeds, water which carries away seeds which do not sink in water—

all these fulfil the wishes of plants. Do you ever pause to think, my friend, that you are fulfilling that wish when you pick peaches or other such fruit and throw their pips far away after eating them? Or when you arrive home with sticky plant seeds on you, do you realize that, without being asked, that plant has turned you into its servant who spreads it seeds?

When summer starts, the earth usually wears its green blanket, which soothes people's tired eyes. All of us often admire the beauty of the land. But how many remember that small thing that gives plants that green colour sustains all things that live on this earth? Do you ever pause to think that you would not be able to breathe, had it not been for that little green—not to mention our pride, and wars? For there is no food that plants can make without that little green stuff, together with the sun and air! These three things are the foundation of all things that live on earth.

That is how it is, my friend, genius does not dwell in one species.[2] Even among plants it dwells. One who walks among them with eyes open can see it. For intelligence has been spread all over, and all where we scratch under the surface we discover it; all over we find it as amazing genius which surpasses human understanding. It has been deliberately scattered all over so that it reminds us that at all times there exists the Omniscient One who is the source of all this intelligence that we see. It has been deliberately scattered all over so that one who has eyes can see. It is not in vain that astronomers, botanists and zoologists, physiologists, astronauts and marine biologists—it is not in folly that they eventually fall down, kneeling and praising the power that has created all this, because they feel weak before that intelligence, and their hearts shout like the hearts of those who keep shouting day and night, saying: 'He is

---

2 The author uses a Sotho proverb, which literally translates as 'wisdom does not dwell in one place'.

holy, He is holy, He is holy, Jehovah of Hosts; the whole world is full of His glory!'

MONEY

The other day I was thinking about a matter that ended up making me laugh all by myself. I had a lot of money, and I put it in my pocket. After that I went out into the street. I think to those who were looking at me I was just like any other person who was passing by. They did not know that I was carrying three hundred rand— that is, seventy-five herd of cattle—in my pocket. For that is what money is. It symbolizes cattle, sheep, horses, chickens, milk, goats, eggs—and everything that you can buy with it. But it is not often that we think of it that way; we are used to money. Just imagine how difficult it would be if a person were to go to the bank driving a herd of his bulls, and tell them to save them for him! Where would they keep them, grazing what, who would herd them, using them for work where, treated by whom when they are sick, when others have gored one to death what would they say; how would they brand them so that they should know which ones belong to you when you want them (for you would not agree to accept someone's emaciated cattle when you know that yours were sturdy!). Would you really get them quickly when you need them, without having to travel somewhere, far away in a cattle post, where they graze? It would be just confusion, my friend.

But money is different. It stands for everything.

You carry it easily when you go to the bank; they save it easily and spend it, for they know that the day you want it they will give you exactly the same amount that is equivalent to yours, even though perhaps it is not exactly the money you deposited; whenever you want it, you get it (unless you perhaps want thousands and thousands). It does not die, it does not rot, it does not gore another as cows do and it is easily portable. Yes, it is even easily more stealable than cattle! You can count it more easily than cattle. Have you noticed that you cannot teach a person who does not even know where the first letter of the alphabet is facing anything about money? He can count it just as well as you do, even though you may count it faster than him or her.

Just go visit a foreign country and you will see what money is all about. When you get there, among foreigners who speak a strange language, you find yourself lost, without understanding what they are saying, you are just like an idiot; you begin to realize that your currency has no value, it no longer carries the weight that those who know it have given it, it cannot even buy you food; it is despised, it is not known, and it seems to be lost just like you, the owner. No, here you realize that it might have been better if you came driving your herd of calves. But when you get to the bank, you will find those who know your currency, they will take it and give you the currency of the country where you are.

And there you will learn other things about money. You will find that your money is not equal to this country's in value. It may be bigger, maybe smaller. For that is the way of money. I say even in its own country it changes. In some years, four rand is equal to a cow, but at other times that very same cow has the value of twenty or thirty rand! It is very unreliable, and a person who places too much trust in it will age before his time. But on that score, I know that I am talking to myself . . .

*

When a hen that has hatched chicks scratches on the ground, calling its chicks, they go running and jumping over each other, each one hurrying for what it is called for. They do not do that only when they are small, but I say even when they have grown up and are adults. If you do not believe, just take sorghum, and stand on a bare field and call, 'knock knock!' And spread it on the ground, you will see. Cattle are just the same.

People too. It is a shameful thing but it is true. For, my friend, we are not really that superior to these poor animals of God. If you do not believe, just plant money in the street, you will see! Or if you need it, investigate the ways in which we get it, you will see that we jump over each other, trampling on each other, killing each other, shoving each other, ruffling each other up when we are in a hurry for money, like chickens are hurrying for sorghum or maize, or cattle being fed bales of grass.

Money is strong, my friend. Those who know it says that it talks. That is why many people work very hard. It is not that they necessarily like to do so, but they do it so that they can have a little more of it. Some go to the extent of doing certain jobs which their hearts do not like, just because it yields a lot of money. Then we end up with a person who was created to look after cattle working with people. Or we see a doctor roughing up people when he examines them; he should have been a carpenter or stone sculptor but became a doctor because of chasing after money.

I said that many people work hard in pursuit of having a lot of money. But considering most of them, you will find that it is not necessarily true that if you work hard every day, you will have a lot of money. How many go around destroying, carrying heavy loads, running around as messengers, who do laundry the whole day, but only get a few cents? But some who wake up after frost has already melted, who go back home when the shadow of evening sets, collect it in dishfuls. That is surprising if you do not study situations carefully.

But if you think of it hard, you will realize that the latter group, who seem to be getting a lot of money for nothing, work more than the former group, because they work with their heads; and one who works with his or her head does not get rest except only in sleep, because even after leaving the place of work the head still wrestles with work matters. Perhaps even at night they keep him or her insomniac, he or she does not sleep well. That is why they age fast. Even when he or she is with his or her children, he or she keeps thinking about these matters. His or her children do not find time to play with him or her, as they should. They are like orphans while he or she is still alive! No, such self-sacrifice must be rewarded well.

But these things are not clear in people's eyes. To some, money is something that is only ill gotten, but not through hard work. Some end up not working at all, looking at many possible crooked ways of getting a lot of money in a short space of time. They break into shops, steal and sell. They run around this country looking for marijuana to buy from those who think that it is lucrative to plant fields of marijuana instead of sorghum or maize or corn. They get chased, get shot and they overturn in vehicles, and they die. Some steal gold or diamond; some are cattle thieves, they go around raking other people's cattle and sheep from cattle ranches, or go shearing sheep that belong to other people when the price of wool is good.

As for those, their criminality is blue collar and can be detected. Some of the money hunters are hiding their criminality in their hearts—which is one of the talents that human beings are endowed with. Such criminality is also found in churches. New ones are founded and a myriad of reasons is given, whereas the main reason is only to make money. Even in some of the established churches, the situation is the same. The congregation always give many offerings, and over and above that we grew up knowing, which was means to advance missionary work. Even in families this malpractice exists. There are young women (and young men) who want to marry only where there is plenty of money, or where they think that there is plenty of money. Some of them, when they think that it has rained money and the poor husband has filled the house with furniture, rake everything and escape while the man is at work. Others, when they realize that where they thought there was plenty of money, things are tough, the road is going uphill with difficulties, jump ship and go ahead where they can reap the fruit of trees that they did not cultivate or even irrigate. Some are unfortunate. Their husbands do not live long; they become widows twice or three times. But yes, there is money because these men die after they had paid their debts, of mortgages or vehicle hire purchases or immovable properties. It seems they know when death is close, because most of them die after they bequeathed their properties to their wives.

You would think that when a person has made a lot of money he would rest, and relax. No. A greedy person, who has made money in several ways, straight and crooked, lives in fear all the time. He is scared of other people because he thinks that they are thinking of snatching it from him in the same way that he snatched it from others. For the sin that you commit against someone will consume you, because all the time you will be thinking that others are waiting to commit it against you. Thus, a person who has made money that way lives bereft of peace, without rest at heart, without sleeping properly, suffering from stomach aches all the time until he has ulcers, or is afflicted by heart aches or become mad. Some go to the extent of committing suicide when they think that they may be robbed of their money and fall back to poverty.

There are some who have a lot of money, who know how to rest, to relax: who live in peace without fear that it may disappear; who are not scared of their fellow men because they did not cheat them. In most cases, these are people who kept doing their work diligently without placing their hearts much on money; they simply regard it as something that they make a living with but not what they live for. As far as they are concerned, the fear that the money that they have saved may disappear does not feature at all. In saving it, they are only preparing for their children or days of old age. While they are still alive, just working, they have no fear and they therefore live long. The money that they have saved increases and it gains interest where it is, it follows those words that say: 'Each will be given according to what he has.'[1]

I say that they live in peace because they live for noble purposes; they live to fulfil any work that they are created for, which satisfies their souls, which is the talent that they are given. As far as they are concerned, money is only the reward for that work, the sweat of their brows. They do not live for it; they live for that work to fulfil their humanity. For what is using your talent if not to fulfil your humanity? Money gained in that way is laudable. One who is wealthy that way deserves respect. But most of us think that it is any money that calls for respect. Therefore, they live only for it.

---

1 A paraphrase of Romans 12:6: 'We have different gifts, according to the grace given to each of us.'

MARRIAGE

There are things which cause laughter, and one of them is when the elders of a young man and those of a young woman meet for negotiating marriage.[1] The young woman's father already knows the matter that has brought the guests to his homestead, perhaps he has seen their son visiting his house over a few months, but visiting his sons, not her. Perhaps he even knows his handwriting because letters used to arrive every day, addressed to his daughter. Perhaps he and his wife have discussed this matter, and the young woman's mother spoke to her about this matter. Maybe they were worried when they saw weeks turning into months and months turning into a year, thinking that this boy is wasting their daughter's time. Today they have come, and what do we get?

The young woman's mother is very excited and just waiting to hear how much *bohadi*[2] is going to be, so that she can go around the village telling other women how well her daughter has been married, so that they cajole their daughters about this matter, and keep saying:

---

1 The author uses a Sotho idiomatic expression: 'to ask for a calabash of water'. The calabash in this context is a symbolic reference to the woman whose hand is being asked for in marriage.
2 Cattle given to the bride's family. In time, the cattle was replaced by money.

'This child is a moron! She will never fetch twenty herd of cattle for her marriage, like Dimakatso.' The same applies to the daughter. She is happy in her heart because today she is about to become a wife, she will be regarded with respect by other women; she has evaded a title that scares Basotho maidens—spinster.[3] Yes, today the maiden feels like a person who is entering heaven, for as far as they are concerned, marriage is not the beginning of difficult life which demands work. As far as they are concerned, marriage is the end of a difficult life which demands work . . . to find a husband.

But the young girl's husband has changed. He is now sad. Even though the boy's family are people that he knows, today he is treating them like strangers. Today he is talking like a king. He is sulking, as if he will lose cattle if he does not behave that way. He is agitated; they have come to disturb him, even though tomorrow they will be pleasantly calling each other *mokgotsi* or *mokgwenyana*.[4] But today they will be arguing about the number of cattle. Yes, eventually they will come to an agreement, and conclude everything by drinking beer, and part happily.

The appointed day is advancing, and joy grows because a wedding has a way of making many people happy, not to mention the groom and the bride. Their elders feel very fortunate now that their children are marrying each other properly, and they are already imagining themselves carrying grandchildren in the future. The young man's relatives invite each other to attend their child's wedding, feeling that they are people to reckon with and now they have a chance to show off because this is their feast. They work very hard, and even those who were not on good terms have reconciled.

---

3 The word for spinster in Sesotho is *lefetwa*: 'one who has been passed by'. Of course, it is heavily loaded with derogatory connotations.

4 *Mokgotsi* is a name that the bride and groom's parents used to refer to each other. Literally meaning 'friend', in this context it also connotes new blood ties.

For a wedding really brings people together, not only those whose children are getting married to each other but even those who help with the wedding. Everywhere in the village, people are singing in preparation for the great day that is coming.

*

My dear Sello

Yesterday we attended Dipuo's wedding. When the bell rang, we were already seated in our places. Oh, the wedding guests were so sprucely dressed! They were dressed to kill; in costumes that some of us were seeing for the first time, and it showed that they had well prepared for that day! I think it was because of the general saying that people 'are seen' at their best on such occasions.

When the time came, the woman who was playing the organ started playing it beautifully, her eyes fixed on the entrance. When the bride stepped on the threshold, she played a traditional wedding song. We all stood up, we twisted our necks to an extent that they became sore, just to see how she was dressed. Dipuo stepped in, treading slowly as if she was reluctant to do so, she was chocolate-coloured, and more beautiful than usual. Wearing a trousseau whiter than snow. Maiden started whispering: 'Look how beautiful Dipuo is, Hey people!'

I was looking at Dipuo with my eyes but in my heart, I saw you and me, my dear, the day our day arrives. I can imagine a church full of people who have come to watch us, craning their necks to see how we are dressed! I can imagine us standing in front of the reverend, answering questions, taking an oath . . . I really smiled to myself when I saw Dipuo and hers standing in front of the reverend.

But even though Dipuo and her beloved were a good match, I do not think that they will live peacefully. I know Dipuo; we grew up together. But that is not our business, to see how they manage. As for me, I know that I will live in peace with mine at all times, isn't it so? After the wedding ceremony was done at the church, there was great partying at home. Many photos were taken, and we ate and sang. In the evening, presents were given, there were speeches, but some people like talking without end! Some people got tired of those speeches because people usually go to a wedding to go out and get things that can make them happy and enjoy themselves. They go there to dance or sing. Most are not even bothered about whom they are dancing for, or whom they are singing for. They don't care whether the people who are getting married will wake up or not the next day, all they care about is to get the opportunity to dance or sing. I think that when we attend weddings, we actually do not go there for the sake of the marrying couple, we do not go there to rejoice with them. We go there for our own sake, to be merry.

People dispersed late at night. The couple left the following day. But I hear that Dipuo was not even crying . . . she was not sad for leaving her home. Yes, but on that score, I don't see any fault in her. How can a person cry when she is going where she likes? What worries me is what Puleng told me.

She says Dipuo said that there were some members of the groom's family who were talking too much when they were given final advices,[5] casting aspersions at her. She was

---

5 It is a custom among the Basotho and other Bantu peoples that, on the evening of the wedding, both families sit with the newly weds and impart advice about married life. The word used for this is *ho lauwa*—literally, 'to be warned'.

really upset by this and would get even with them if 'they ever visit' her place! That's really bad.

That is all about Dipuo's wedding, my dear. I feel dizzy with joy when I think that one day it will be you and I, and someone will be writing to her beloved this way when you and I will be husband and wife.

From,

Your beloved,

TLALENG

*

'Here is a letter, *Ntata* Dipuo. It has just arrived.'

'Oh! I thought you were busy behind the hut?'

'No, I have just arrived. Did you hear the car that was idling outside? It brought Puleng to her home. She is so chubby. She is carrying a baby boy and has come home to rest, in accordance with the Sotho custom. Oh, I really see that they have established a real family and marriage is smiling on here. Her mother is so excited, poor woman!'[6]

'Yes, that's good. I will also see her later. I wonder where Moloi is, I would like him to come and read this letter for me.' *Mma* Dipuo goes out and after a few minutes she comes back with Moloi. The letter is opened and Moloi reads it: 'Father and Mother. I am fine here. I am sure you are surprised because of not hearing from me. No, it is not because am sick, but it is because of reasons that you will hear soon.

'I regret to tell you that Selemo and I are no longer living together. There is no use for me to go on explaining the reasons

---

6 In this context, the phrase 'poor woman' is used to express admiration and not pity.

that caused this. But we were no longer living in peace and we decided that it would be better if we separated. I know that this will break your hearts, because you will think that I am sad. But that is not so. Now I am out of sadness. Therefore, I ask you not to be worried—why should you be sad when we, the people who are concerned, are not sad . . . ?

Dipuo's elders were no longer able understand what followed next. Their hearts were broken. Tears were flowing down *Mma* Dipuos's cheeks. As for the old man, he was just staring in front of him, without saying a word. Even when Moloi said goodbye he did not hear him. He began to answer when *Mma* Dipuo asked a painful question, crying, obviously in sorrow:

'What wrong has my child committed; why is she so unfortunate? Why is she not like the likes of Puleng?'

'No, don't talk that way, *mme*, you know that marriage is only a matter of luck. It is like when a person is standing where roads diverge, where he has to choose. Maybe he chooses a path that he thinks has been paved, is smooth, but when he has finished a day on it, finds that is full of terrible farrows, which have no bridge.

'Maybe he chooses a beautiful path, which is smooth, but digs holes in it as he goes along, walking on it like a ploughing going through a field. That's where roads diverge . . . '

They heard voices of people passing by outside, which kept saying: 'Hello Dimakatso dear! You look so chubby! This child is well married, *basadi*!' In their hearts, Radipuo[7] and his wife were thinking of the wedding day, thinking of its beauty, wondering whether on that day there was anyone who could imagine that this would happen . . . !

---

7 Dipuo's father, same as *Ntata* Dipuo.

OLD AGE

When we are still small, we usually worry about future matters, about next year, about things that are coming. We wish to grow up, to become men and women who have families. We only look ahead; we do not want to look back because behind us progress is still very small, there is nothing that has been done. That is why a child likes it when people call it 'grandfather' or 'grandmother'. This helps them to come closer to the year that that they like, where their eyes are facing. But when life approaches its end, we look where progress is advanced, we wish to look at our works; we are reluctant to look ahead, to see where the valley of the shadow of death is awaiting us, because we know that it is very close. We wish to go back to childhood when old age arrives.

It is not just a wish. We actually do go back in various ways. We become physically weak. Muscles that were strong, biceps that were beautiful, huge necks, big calves, all disappear, and the only evidence that is left is the wrinkled skin that once covered muscular parts, even though now you are just like a child. When a person walks, it is as if it is a child walking, tottering along, who has become just a flabby thing. When he tries to jump over a fence, he faces the difficulty of childhood. Trying to eat is a problem; food verges on throttling him because the mouth is smooth inside. When he swallows, he gulps noisily. Water must always be at hand so that he can wash down the piece of meat that might choke him. The voice is now weak, eyes can no longer see properly, and memory is also weak.

But just pay them a visit in that state, my friend; they will start telling a story which you will never forget, a story that will sometime make you laugh a lot; yes, some of them will make you feel sad, and make tears flow down your face.

'Oh, teacher my child, you see us, weak as we are today, but we were strong people in our days. We were healthy young men and women. Don't you undermine your mother here, she was a light-complexioned beauty, with whom all men fell head over heels in love. Even the day when I went to propose love to her, my friends said that I was just going to waste my time, how was I going to manage a person who was so spoilt for choice of men every day? (The old lady smiled). Even though she is smiling, that was indeed how it was in those days. Yes, we argued seriously, teacher, and there were young men that we grew up with. Do you still remember them, Mmatlhoriso? Letsatsi and company, Hlakodi, Putswe . . . '

'*Ntata* Tlhoriso, you know, I always remind you to respect the souls of the departed!'

The old man kept quiet for a moment. I saw droplets of tear in his eyes. I saw clearly that he was far away, in those olden days; imagining himself with his friends when they were still alive. He could not have imagined them that way without thinking that they are now departed. The thought that they are no more shook his feelings like a person who was awoken from a dream in which he was in the company of people that he loved but who are no longer here. He only said: 'It's true, teacher, they left us.' Then he kept quiet, and it seemed he was not going to continue. I was at a loss for a few minutes, but before I could clear my throat the old lady took up the thread of the story where the old man left off.

117

'I see all those days, teacher, but as far as I am concerned, the one that stands out as if it were yesterday is the wedding day, my child. You are looking at the wall. In our days, photos did not exist, but I really don't forget that day. To me it seems like yesterday. We did not wear these modern flashy clothes . . . ' At this point, my thoughts started wandering and I started thinking about the fashion of olden days as I have seen them in paintings, that one now sees in magazines. I was surprised because it was the first time that I realized that those days were just as colourful as ours; those clothes that we find funny, to them they were as beautiful as today's.

'Yes, it was truly a pleasant feast, my child. At the end, after we were united into one by the reverend, he read a hymn and concluded with the following words:

' . . . They must reach the end of the road

Still in love;

So that they should not leave each other behind

When they reach You . . . '

I felt like weeping for joy. And here it is, today we have reached that very end.'

When she finished, she looked at me with eyes that seemed to be asking whether I and the one that I will choose for myself . . . will reach the end of the road together. Those eyes were heavy; it was as if they were judging me, not only me but me and my generation. I heard myself asking a question to blunt the sharpness of those eyes.

'Did you have children?'

'Yes, teacher, we were blessed with children and some of them are still alive.' She paused there; I was also shedding tears and I realized that their thoughts were making them sad, they evoked emotions that they were unable to bear. My friends, my friends . . . at times it seems as if it is said, 'I will visit the sins of the children upon their parents.'[1]

Right now I was seeing only one thought in the mind of these two old folks, I could see that they hankered for one thing that they wished could be given to them—to be young again; and I saw that if it could be given to them and they were told that they should choose again, they would choose the same path and walk with each other with love as they have already done. But now the end was nigh. There was one thing that bothered them. They knew that in the future one of them will have to leave the other behind with sorrowful thoughts of what has gone by, and that one will be redeemed by death. That thought also brought tears to their eyes, because they were used to helping each other carry loads, and each felt sad when he or she thought that the beloved might remain behind in sorrow, without anyone to console him or her. They placed their trust in death, that it would eventually reunite them again, and for that matter they prayed that it should do so soon and very soon.

---

1 The author paraphrased and changed 'the sins of the fathers shall be visited upon the sons' (Exodus 20:14) to 'I shall visit the sins of the children upon their parents.'

THE END

When a person is on a journey, there are things that are discouraging, that drain his strength, that make a person feel like going back to where he comes from. One of them is being overtaken by a car that is running at high speed, which makes a pedestrian feel that he is doing nothing but simply playing. This is discouraging because when he looks back, he sees the dust of a vehicle, rising where he passed earlier on, in the morning, but before he crosses the river it passes at high speed and overtakes him, throwing dust in his eyes. When he looks ahead where it disappeared, and ponders as to when he is going to get there, he feels discouraged.

What discourages him is when he sees that the way he is walking he will not reach the end of the road. That is, the road looks as if it has no end. That is the case when a road is straight, which you find stretching ahead of you when you appear on every hillock. Even a road that has no villages on either side is similar, because villages seem to break a road into several segments and one does not feel every segment when he walks its distance. These segments are encouraging because one reaches the end of every segment quickly.

The same applies to books. A very long book also discourages us. We become lazy to start reading it because we see that its end is very far. What might encourage us is when it has chapters that are not too long, because they may deceive us and make us forget its length, and think instead about the beginning and end of every chapter.

The end is something that is necessary. There aren't many things that we would start if we did not know that the end is not that far. We know how pleasant it is to start something. It is equally pleasant to reach the end. Just think about the end of a journey. Maybe the muscles are now weak, or the feet are now swollen, and your clothes are heavy on the shoulders, your head is aching because of the sun, hunger has also thrown in its lot, and thirst. But these no longer bother you because you have reached the end of your journey, you will rest, massage your muscles, eat, be full, quench your thirst, sleep and rest. Yes, now you will narrate and tell others what you saw on the road: pleasant and painful things. They will listen to you till night falls. You will narrate again the next day, and days will pass that way. You will rest and after months you will start planning another journey.

The same applies to books. When you approach the end, you rejoice because your eyes are about to rest, and the neck that you have bent for a long time. You reach the end, you close it, you shut your eyes; you think about things that you read in it, you ponder over them, it is only then that they are settling well in your mind, it is only then that you understand what the author intended you to understand, it is only then that they satisfy your heart or your soul. You start talking about that book to your friends. You feel that you have found something new. Indeed, reading is something very important . . . you are already on the way to start another interesting book when you think that way.

But you will realize that the kind of end that we have talked about is not eternal. It comes only when the body needs to take a break because it is weak; not that the spirit is exhausted. The spirit does not get exhausted. Every day it wants to go ahead, but it is only held back by this weak body. The heart is willing (that is, the spirit) but the flesh is weak. When the body has rested, the end that we thought is the end comes to an end, like a village by the roadside, where we take a detour when we are tired, hungry and thirsty. We just take a detour, the road does not end there and when we have rested, we start again. It was only a passing end, for the real end, my friend, is something that we dread, it is something that is very painful, which disturbs our feelings. Have you ever felt sadness in your heart when a train whistles, whistling, when it announces that it is entering your home station, whistling and announcing that you now have to part with travellers that you have long been travelling with, who have become your new friends, whistling and announcing that you will no longer listen to the wheels of the train under you? Or when you finish an interesting book, have you ever felt that it should not end? Have you realized that when it ends you part with these many people that you found in its pages, people that you knew and understood, that you loved like anyone that you know, maybe you loved them more than those that you know? Now when you reach the end of a book, that is, the end of your friendship with them, the end of their lives (because they live only in the book), have you felt how painful it is?

That is how painful it is, my compatriot, when any friendship comes to an end. Whether it ends because of a quarrel, or parting or death. We usually feel that we are losing something great. When we part because of a quarrel or a journey or migration, we usually have hope that we will meet again. But if it is death, we usually see that we are defeated, but quickly realize that it only takes away this, our weak flesh, which weighs on the spirit. For after death the spirit remains, which is our part that brings us very close to the Creator, a part that does not know exhaustion, which knows no end, for it is a part of the one who knows the beginning and the end, because he is the alpha and the omega.